Growing Up in Toronto "The Good"

Growing Up in Toronto
"The Good"

by
Sheila Craig Waengler

IGUANA

Copyright © 2024 Sheila Craig Waengler
Published by Iguana Books
720 Bathurst Street
Toronto, ON M5S 2R4

All rights reserved. No part of this publication may be reproduced, stored in a retrieval system or transmitted, in any form or by any means, electronic, mechanical, recording or otherwise (except brief passages for purposes of review) without the prior permission of the author.

Publisher: Cheryl Hawley
Editor: Beth Kaplan

ISBN 978-1-77180-700-5 (black-and-white paperback)
ISBN 978-1-77180-709-8 (colour paperback)
ISBN 978-1-77180-701-2 (epub)

This is an original print edition of *Growing Up in Toronto "The Good"*.

Family Tree of Sheila Craig Waengler

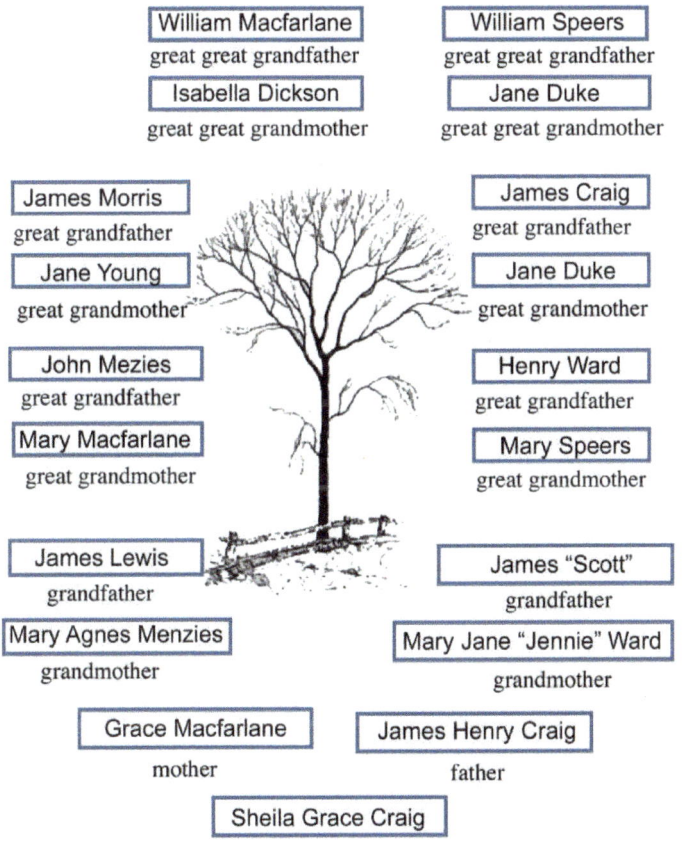

William Macfarlane	William Speers
great great grandfather	great great grandfather
Isabella Dickson	Jane Duke
great great grandmother	great great grandmother

James Morris	James Craig
great grandfather	great grandfather
Jane Young	Jane Duke
great grandmother	great grandmother
John Mezies	Henry Ward
great grandfather	great grandfather
Mary Macfarlane	Mary Speers
great grandmother	great grandmother

James Lewis	James "Scott"
grandfather	grandfather
Mary Agnes Menzies	Mary Jane "Jennie" Ward
grandmother	grandmother

Grace Macfarlane	James Henry Craig
mother	father

Sheila Grace Craig

by: James Bruce Craig
my nephew.

Preface

My ancestors all came from Scotland. For the most part, they were Celts, the Highlanders. One branch only had their roots in Normandy. They were Lowland Scots and were tolerant of their English rulers. The Highlanders wanted the pretender Charles Edward Lewis John Sylvester Maria Casimir Stuart (born 1722 in Rome and died in 1788 in the Vatican) better known as "Bonny" Prince Charlie to be their King. They resented the English dominance. They were triumphant in battle against the English when they used surprise tactics such as attacking the redcoats from the hills. However, these bold clansmen were no match against the Hanoverian and English forces when "Bonny" Prince Charlie egged them on to fight the disciplined Hanoverian and English on the flat field at Culloden. They were greatly outnumbered and suffered a disastrous defeat. Many clan chieftains were slain. When I visited in my eighties there were huge marker stones naming clan chieftains, lairds who died in the battle. The clans were decimated and never recovered fully.

My great-great-great-great-great grandfather, John Speers, on my father's side was one of the rebellious Jacobites who barely escaped after the battle of Culloden in a rowboat to Northern Ireland with the Brits hot on his tail. These brave Scots who fought for an independent Scotland are still under English rule. Two generations of the Speers family lived in Ireland. Thomas Speers, a grandson of John Speers, was born in 1778 in County Armagh. In 1828 with his wife, Anne Dodds, and all of their children, some in their young adult years, Thomas travelled from Northern Ireland on a sailing ship to Canada, likely landing first at Quebec City. The Speers family then made their way to Upper Canada (Ontario) and settled in Caledon Township. Land was cleared and a farm established on a hundred-acre lot on the southwest corner of Airport Road and the Caledon Sideroad.

William Speers, born in 1802 in Northern Ireland, is the eldest son of Thomas Speers and Anne Dodds. William was married to Jane Duke in Northern Ireland and travelled with his wife and all of the Speers family to Canada in 1828. William and Jane also settled in Caledon Township and cleared land for a farm of their own. In the 1850s, as land was opening up for farms in Grey County and Bruce County, about 150 kilometres to the northwest of Caledon, William and Jane and their family moved to Keppel Township, Grey County, located just to the east of Wiarton. They had a daughter, Mary Speers, in 1837. Mary married Henry Ward, born in 1836. Sometime after 1861 the family moved north to Owen Sound in Grey County. Mary Jane married James Scott Craig. They had three children, Mamie Craig, James Henry Craig, and Evelyn Craig. Mamie died at the age of two. James Craig, my father, was born in 1888 and died in 1954.

Father's Grandfather Craig and family—his wife, Mary Jane, my father as a small boy, and my Aunt Evelyn, his little sister.

My Aunt Evelyn, my grandmother, and my grandfather en route to church.

My father's early upbringing in Owen Sound caused him stress all his life. His parents were brought up as Anglicans but when they moved from the farm in Caledon to Owen Sound, they discovered that the Methodist church was the only church. They attended it faithfully with their son, James, and his younger sister, Evelyn. It was the town where my father told me he took a Bible to school in kindergarten, for which he was rewarded by getting the strap, and the next year given the strap for not bringing a Bible to school. This was the town that frowned upon anyone drinking a glass of beer. It was the last town in Ontario to permit the selling of any alcoholic beverage. This was as late as 1972.

***

I have records of my mother's peaceful forefathers on the male side. George Morris, born in 1754, and his wife Janet Grey, came from Paisley and were involved in the shawl industry. Their son James was born in 1782. The paisley shawl industry was in trouble in the 1820s, and James's silk and wool manufacturing business failed, mainly due to Napoleonic wars. So, with his eleven-year-old son, bankrupt, leaving his wife and other children behind, set sail for Canada. They settled in the Ottawa Valley ,in the Township of MacNab, early in 1829. His wife, Mary Wright, and his other children followed. They had to deal with the harsh, unforgiving elements as well as a very demanding and domineering Laird of MacNab. After clearing the heavy hardwood forests, they entered the lumber industry and were successful.

In 1846 my great-grandfather James Morris of McNab became the first Registrar for the County of Renfrew. Prior to that, the first post office in the county was in James Morris's home. In 1853 his son became Registrar and in 1866 he also became Sheriff.

When the school of engineering was first introduced at the U of T, my grandfather James L. Morris was the first and only graduate. While at university he would have his laundry done north of the city, in the Village of Yorkville. As a young surveyor, he assisted in laying out the townsites of Sudbury and Calgary. Unlike some others, this principled young man refused to accept some of his pay in grants of land near or in the proposed centres of these towns. During his life, he negotiated and recorded a number of treaties with the Indian tribes of Ontario. The Department of Lands and Forests published his collection in the form of a book, "Indians of Ontario." By this time, he had an honorary degree, Doctor of Engineering. In his eighties, he shot the rapids in a canoe.

My maternal grandparents were a loving couple. Grandmother's descendants were the Celtic Macfarlane clan of the Isle of Skye and the peaceful clan of Menzies of Weem, Scotland. The Menzies' roots were Norman rather than Celtic. Scotland is indebted to the Menzies, who brought the larch tree from the Austrian Tirol in 1737 and presented it to the Duke of Athol, who introduced it to Scotland where it flourished.

6 Growing Up in Toronto "The Good"

Grandfather James Morris and Grandmother Mary Macfarlane Menzies Morris, mother's parents. A truly loving couple.

My grandmother's first Canadian ancestor was Isabella Dickson, who was born in Dalkeith, Midlothian, Scotland. Accompanied by her brother, the ships doctor on the crossing, she emigrated to Upper Canada, married William Macfarlane, and they operated an inn with the tavern in Packenham. Isabella had five children. When her husband died, she became known as the "Widow Macfarlane" in Packenham. In time she became one of the prominent landowners. During the rebellion of 1837, the Orangeman were suspicious of the Highlanders and organized marches on those of Scottish ancestry in the region. The Highlanders retreated to the widow Macfarlane's tavern, and a twenty-four-hour battle ensued. Some of the projectiles, including frying pans, caused a few serious injuries. Isabella "the widow Macfarlane" died in 1862, and her daughter Mary Agnes married John Menzies in Almonte (now Mississippi).

Mary Macfarlane, known as the "widow Lady Macfarlane." Painted by my grandmother, Mary Agnes.

Almonte house on the Mississippi River in the town of Mississippi—formerly the town of Almonte.

They had three children who lived through adulthood. John Basil Menzies became a doctor in Quebec and froze to death attempting to reach a patient when his wagon wheel got entangled in a root in the forest en route. A second son moved out west, and their sister, my grandmother Mary Macfarlane, lived from 1861 to 1947. Grandmother grew up in Almonte and died in Toronto. My great-uncle Robert Macfarlane, a lawyer located in Stratford, Ontario, became the Liberal MP for his riding in the Canada West Parliament, and my grandmother attended the inaugural ball.

My mother was Grace Macfarlane Morris, born in the town of Pembroke, Ontario, some hundred and forty-five kilometres (ninety miles) north of Ottawa and only five kilometres from the Quebec border. Her family with their Scottish background attended the Presbyterian church in Pembroke. Some of Mother's close friends were "The Budore girls" who were French Canadians from Quebec and Roman Catholic. Mother may have had her faults, but she was no bigot.

Mother's brother, my uncle Basil, fought in the First World War (28 July 1914 to 11 November 1918), a global conflict between two coalitions: the Allies and the Central Powers. Fighting took place throughout Europe, the Middle East, Africa, the Pacific and parts of Asia. One of the deadliest wars in history, it resulted in an estimated 9 million soldiers dead and 23 million wounded plus up to 8 million civilian deaths from numerous causes including genocide. The move of large numbers of troops and civilians during the war was a major factor in spreading the 1918 Spanish flu pandemic.

My mother with brothers Ramsey (on her right) and Basil (on her left).

After spending almost three years in the mud and horror of the trenches, Uncle Basil couldn't take it any longer. Not wanting to die in those conditions, he applied and was accepted by the Brits in the Royal Flying Corp. (The Royal Canadian Airforce was not as yet established.) It was common knowledge that the average life expectancy for the airmen was probably three months. The planes were very flimsy and could be knocked down with a minor hit. Parachutes were not yet part of the equipment, Basil was assigned to a fighter plane as an observer. On one such flight, after flying over the enemy lines, the plane was hit and Basil was wounded on crash landing. The second time he was not so lucky and was killed.

World War I Royal Flying Corps Fighter plane and pilot.

Part 1

Sheila Craig, 1930–1947

Chapter 1

I wouldn't say Toronto was an innocent city back in 1930, but it was small, and I was very small. I was born less than six months before the great stock market crash in October of 1929. My father was forty and my mother was thirty-nine. From the Wellesley Hospital, my parents brought me home to Dawlish Avenue, to the house my architect father had designed and built. It was completed in 1926, just in time for the birth of their first living child, Jimmy, to arrive in April of that year. My sister, Mary, arrived in August 1928. Two perfect little blond WASP babies, both planned. I was not. My parents were going to call me Angela if I was a girl, but when they saw my head of black hair, they decided that name wasn't suitable, since, I assume, they thought no one with black hair would be sufficiently angelic to warrant the name. So I was called Sheila.

The Depression was well underway in 1930. In later years, around the dinner table, Father told the family how, back in early 1929, there had been a very imaginative plan to redesign University Avenue, which would terminate in a stunning treatment of the waterfront, taking advantage of Toronto's ideal situation on beautiful Lake Ontario with its natural harbour and the Toronto islands acting as a buffer. Sadly, this plan never materialized because, a few months later, the Great Depression happened, it seemed overnight.

Perhaps you didn't know that Toronto "The Good," as it was known at the time, was under the influence of the temperance lobbyists. I never understood why they were called the Temperance Society. Wouldn't the Abolitionist Society be a more suitable name for people who believed that consuming alcohol was sinful? Later in my life, my mother explained that, around the turn of the century, when Canada was still growing into a nation, mining and seasonal forestry were lucrative jobs for young unskilled men who had wives and sometimes young children; they would very often take on seasonal employment up north. However, at the end of the season, when they received their pay, these young men who had worked very hard physically wanted to relax before heading home with their earnings. So, they would go to the local "watering hole," which was a local term used for a bar, and drink with their buddies to celebrate. Sadly, many of them drank away their hard-earned money and went home to their families empty-handed. And that was the main reason why women crusaded for temperance, a term less offensive than abolition.

***

I adored my grandma. She had a twinkle in her eye and a mischievous sense of humour. She grew up in Renfrew County in the town of Almonte. She told me stories of her youth at Ottawa Ladies' College, where the headmistress seemed to care more about the girls' behaviour than their academic achievements. On one occasion this headmistress chastised Grandma, calling to her, "Mary MacFarlane Menzies, refrain from using those clarion tones and behave like a lady."

Her origins from the Isle of Skye in Scotland helped to shape her character and mine. The highland MacFarlanes were a wild lot.

***

Memories of my very early youth are few and fragmented, so I will (you will be glad to hear) only mention a few. I was lying comfortably under a soft blanket in my baby carriage and looking up to see three pairs of eyes all looking down at me. All these ladies were smiling, and I remember the word "cute" repeated. I didn't know if that meant contentment, but since I didn't yet speak, and they all smiled, I smiled back. This was the era when the importance of skin contact and hugging babies close to mommy's and daddy's bare chests was unheard of.

My second clear memory was of the garden at 123 Dawlish Avenue. I was a toddler. The garden was down two steps from the terrace, which led from French doors both from the living room and the dining room. Instead of having the living room and dining room facing the street, which was the conventional design of the day, Father had designed both rooms facing south to take advantage of the southern exposure and the approach to the garden from the house. The lawn was large enough for a small badminton court. When the net was removed and hoops installed in the grass, people played croquet. On either side of the lawn were flower beds with scalloped edges.

My parents were avid amateur gardeners. Mother, who grew up in Pembroke in the early Edwardian era, had a fondness for some wild weeds, and Queen Anne's lace was interspersed with peonies and other perennials. Mother's favourite was the iris. Her iris beds were well known in our area of Lawrence Park, and Mr. Freestone, my favourite Blythwood School teacher in years to come, came to photograph them. I, as a two-year-old, also liked them very much, and when no one was paying much attention, I would toddle into the flower beds and sit amongst the irises. I liked to squeeze their petals and watch them form funny shapes. This was not popular with Mother.

Father holding Mary, with doll, and Jimmy at Christmas 1928.

Essex Car—bought by father just before the advent of the Great Depression. I remember it on Cuthbert Crescent. I am always in the back on the right-hand side, Mary is always the poor middle child in the middle, and Jimmy is on the left in the back seat, where I refused to sit because just above, on the inside roof, was a little bit of mold

Sheila, aged two, in Mother's Garden.

My grandma wanted to keep me amused and busy and to prevent me from being destructive, even though it was entirely unintentional. She had heard of a cat who had just produced a litter and, with my parents' consent, brought me a tiny black kitten. From the moment I saw it, I was in love. I still remember how thrilled I was to have this dear little, soft creature to cuddle. I admired its graceful movements and didn't mind going to bed at night because I knew I would be greeted in the morning by my dear little friend as I came downstairs for breakfast (the kitten was not allowed upstairs).

One sunny morning I came down for breakfast and my kitten wasn't there. I ran out onto the terrace from the living room French doors, calling, "Where are you, my sweet kitty?" Daddy looked very upset and turned away. Mother intervened, saying, "Your kitten was chasing Marshal Saunders's canaries and caught one, which it toyed with and killed, so we had to get rid of the kitten." I couldn't believe my ears. I believe I was in a state of shock because I'm told that I didn't cry (as was expected.) Instead, I slowly walked to the bottom of the garden behind the garage and hid under the blue spruce tree for the next few hours. All I wondered was why Marshal Saunders's canaries were in my kitten's garden when Marshal's house was on the street below ours, and what right did they have to be in our garden where they didn't belong? Eventually, I was told, I had to be forcibly removed from my hiding place. I didn't dare ask what happened to my kitten. I'd remembered what Jimmy and Mary told me about the stray cat that they'd brought in and who then had kittens in the basement and how excited they were, looking forward to seeing them when they woke up the next morning. But when they woke up, Mother told them the kittens died and she thought the mother had eaten them. Evidently, they had all been drowned. Perhaps it's not fair to tell this story about my mother. Apparently, she had been badly scratched by a feral cat as a child and was not fond of cats.

But Mother did like dogs and told us how, as a child, she loved the family Scotch terrier named Pax. Other than this episode, I remember her as a devoted and caring mother. She was under a great deal of stress at the time because the Great Depression was reaching its peak and it looked as if the family was about to lose everything my parents had worked so hard for, including all their assets and even their heavily mortgaged house.

One more cheerful note, I also remember, while we were still at Dawlish, being told I was to be a little bride at a wedding. That was the only time in my early youth I was excited about putting on a dress. And what a dress! It was a tiny wedding dress, and with it, I was to wear new white shoes and a small tiara. This was to be a wedding in Grace Church on-the-Hill, and the bride was the daughter of mother's cousin Margot Cosby. As I walked down the aisle beside a boy a little older than I, whom I had never seen before, dressed as a groom, I was overwhelmed, not only by the church's size and how small I was, but also by how the boy's top hat was much too large for his head. And I wondered if I was really to be married and what was being married anyway. No one had bothered to explain why I was there and why I got to be dressed as a bride, but it made me feel important, so I guessed it was all right.

I remember another time a little over a year before we had to move away from Dawlish Avenue and our family spent a month in a cottage on Lake Simcoe. I was very happy there, but Mother and Mary found it rather embarrassing because I constantly removed all but my underpants whenever I was outdoors. But I really didn't mind wearing my little red bathing suit, which had a top, because the top had bright red and white stripes. One morning I was allowed to join Jimmy, Mary, and other children on the beach, which was very close to the cottage. It formed a crescent shape and we all walked around to the other side.

All the others knew how to swim, but I hadn't been taught yet. There was a sandbar that stretched out into the lake where the water suddenly became quite deep. Mother and Father were on the other side of the beach, which was a distance away but quite visible. They stopped talking to their friends as they saw me slowly walking out on the sandbar, daring myself to go further. I remember knowing that I should stop, but I was fascinated. At the last moment, with Mother almost screaming for me to stop and just as I saw nothing but water in front of me, Jimmy grabbed me and pulled me back. The next morning my parents' friend Jim Mess took me by the arm down to the water and taught me how to dog paddle. In no time I was swimming like a drunken little fish.

Mother decided that it was time for the Craig children, along with two or three friends whose parents had cottages nearby, to put on a play. She chose Lewis Carroll's *Through the Looking Glass*. Jimmy was to play the Mad Hatter, Mary was to play Alice, and the parts of the Red Queen, the White Rabbit, and the Cheshire Cat, etc. were to be played by the other children. I was to play the Dormouse. Because I had no lines and all I had to do was to attempt to stick my head in the teapot, Mother decided that that was a suitable role for me because there wasn't much that I might do to disrupt the scene. We had an audience of eight adults, and I was quite pleased with my first theatrical role.

12 Growing Up in Toronto "The Good"

Jimmy, Mary, and Sheila "The Little Brat."

Mary dressed as Alice in "Alice Through the Looking Glass."

Chapter 2

My father co-owned an architectural firm, Craig and Madill. He was fortunate that he had a perfect partner in Harry Madill. Harry excelled as an administrator. Dad was full of creative ideas and Harry was happy to leave most of the designing to him, so they were a good team. When the Depression hit, they had lots of jobs lined up, but very soon all but a few were cancelled. They got the contract to design a very long pier just west of the city. It was to be called "The Palace Pier" because it would be rather grand and would extend out onto Lake Ontario, dominating the waterfront with a dance hall and boutiques where the citizens could stroll and enjoy the views and the lake and young people could enjoy dancing with a live orchestra. When the project was half finished, the city ran out of funds. Dad's original plan was cut down to half the length. However, it still was rather impressive with its boutiques and open-air dance hall, a favourite place for young people to go dancing to a live orchestra. My university boyfriend, John Howe, and I were two of the young people who danced there. I felt very grown up because John smuggled a mickey of rye whisky to the hall, which we consumed throughout the evening. The Palace Pier lasted well into my adulthood when, sadly, it burnt down.

Palais Pier, on Lake Ontario's waterfront, was designed by James Craig of Craig and Madill Architects.

Father had ten years to build his career after demobilization from the army in 1918. After four years of war, Major Craig returned to a country of peace that, since the Canadian victory at Vimy Ridge, had grown in stature and was recognized as a nation. His partner, Harry, was also an officer in the Canadian Army. The two united and looked forward to a bright future. As partners, they complemented one another. Harry was very diplomatic, even-tempered, and excellent at negotiations, which was vital, and he had a charming way with clients, especially with bureaucrats. Although Father was likable, he was not always diplomatic. He was intolerant of excessive regulations and, unfortunately, tended to rub minor bureaucrats the wrong way, so Harry was the one to deal with City Hall. Harry handled the office and hired staff, Father designed, and the small firm thrived and looked forward to a bright future that included designing government buildings. One such project was the post office half of the huge building on Front Street that houses the Union Station. In those nine years after the war, Craig and Madill had built a reputation for excellence and were not short of clients.

As well as designing government buildings, including schools, my father had a desire to own real estate, especially since he was married in 1923 and almost immediately started a family. He met a builder who asked him to go into partnership and design an apartment building for a lot that he had recently bought. The builder was able to negotiate a second lot, so Dad designed two apartment buildings, one at the northeast corner of St. Clair Avenue and Avenue Road, facing the corner park with the fountain, and one on the northwest corner of Edmund Avenue and Avenue Road, fronting Edmund Avenue. The apartment buildings were built, but Father's half share was heavily mortgaged.

Feeling flush with the success of the apartment buildings and with his growing family, father bought a 1928 Essex car.

James Craig Senior, my grandfather, had been the manager of a substantial insurance company and was responsible for a large section of Eastern Ontario until the end of the Great War, "the war to end all wars" as the winning side liked to call it. After the armistice, his insurance company refused to pay out life insurance to the widows of men killed on active service. Somewhere in the small print, they found a disclaimer.

My grandfather was so incensed that he resigned and forfeited his considerable pension. However, Dad had designed and, with his parents, had built a duplex at the corner of Cuthbert Crescent and Carey Road, so the Craig seniors moved there from their sizeable house in Parkdale, where they had lived since 1895, the year they moved from Owen Sound. Parkdale at the time was the Rosedale of Toronto. It continued to be a popular residential district until the Gardiner Expressway cut through the area, at which time that elegant old community was destroyed.

***

As the Depression reached its peak in about 1933, Father could not pay the heavy mortgage payments on his equity in 150 St. Clair West and Edmund Avenue. Sadly, for him, he lost his half share in both buildings as well as two houses on Huron Street that he owned jointly with his parents. When both his parents had passed away by the end of 1931, their duplex became available. The family lawyer, Arthur Fleming, had a client from Montreal who was moving to Toronto and needed a house. My parents realized that they were about to lose their family home. The house at 123 Dawlish would fit the bill for the Montreal family, and Cuthbert Crescent would accommodate our family.

Mother was so relieved not to permanently lose her home and her lovely south garden with prize irises, that she didn't complain. The mortgage payments and the taxes would be covered. The duplex was on a small corner lot had a dark little garden. Jimmy, Mary, and I were quite enchanted with a strange piece of equipment that originated in the basement under the main floor kitchen. It was called a dumbwaiter, and a pulley sent it all the way up to the attic with a shelf on the first and second floors. They could save many trips up and down the stairs. I don't know why dumbwaiters went out of style. I think they are a great idea.

Relatively poor ourselves, our parents still trained us to respect those poorer. As young as I was, I still remember when the doorbell rang, it was usually some poor hungry man offering to do any job for the price of a sandwich. Undoubtedly many veterans were suffering from post-traumatic stress disorder and were unemployable, and young people freshly out of high school were often unable to find any work. Many could be observed sleeping in ravines. Mother had a cleaning lady, Mrs. Sara White, who lived a few blocks away. She would come once a week to clean and do the ironing. One day she burst into tears and told our mother that her son Cliff was distraught and was planning to ride the rails (as this dangerous means of transportation was called) west in search of employment of any kind because his mother earned so little and there wasn't enough money to feed him. When Father heard this, he decided to help; he hired Cliff and paid him just enough to buy his food. As it turned out, Cliff was a bright lad, eager to learn, and he did. He eventually became office manager and loyally stayed with the firm, even after my dad died in 1954, until Jimmy left the firm some years later to work in Ottawa with a new partner. Cliff then left Craig and Madill and retired with a clear conscience.

Dad was so disturbed by the terrible unemployment situation for young men that he came up with a plan. He went to Ottawa and proposed that the government sponsor the building of cheap accommodation and small houses and duplexes, and they would hire the unemployed youth to build them. This was just before American President Franklin Delano Roosevelt came up with his New Deal to speed up the end of the Depression. The government in Ottawa was not impressed, and they spread the word that Craig was a "parlour pink," a term they used to describe someone with socialist sympathies.

Dad got the job to build a mausoleum near Uxbridge for the then mayor of Toronto. It would be called the Thomas Foster Memorial and would be the final resting place for Thomas and his wife.

Thomas Foster Memorial Uxbridge, Ontario, designed by James Craig (Craig and Madill Architects).

The family was still living at Cuthbert Crescent when Christmas was approaching. Our parents said that we should make up a large basket for a very poor family that Sara White's daughter, Doris, knew. So we gathered all our old toys. Jimmy repaired the broken ones. Mary, who in later life became an occupational therapist, was very creative in turning a mess into something attractive. I was thrilled when she allowed me to paint the yellow part of a large wooden duck on wheels that Jimmy had laboriously put together and was getting a second life. Mother, who was rather cerebral and practical, decided to donate a large ham with the bone rather than a turkey because it would supply the large family with several substantial meals instead of only one dinner. This did not go over too well with the recipients, who wanted only turkey.

Now I must confess I was and probably still am a bit of a rebellious handful. Jimmy was old enough to understand that our family had come down in the world, and he was upset about having to leave his friends in Lawrence Park. He was easily given to anger accordingly, and his little sister was a bit of a brat and a tease. Because I didn't have a doll, except for a little rubber one, my parents decided to splurge and bought me a beautiful big doll with a porcelain face. Perhaps they thought that would civilize me and make me more feminine. I called her Graceyossa after my mother Grace. But I was not fond of Graceyossa. I much preferred my little rubber doll, Johnny Craig. Mother had made several little suits for him, and he even had his initials embroidered on his shirts. One day, when I was teasing Jimmy, he completely lost his temper and threw Graceyossa down the attic stairs. Poor Graceyossa's porcelain head was smashed. Jimmy felt very badly, as did Mother. I may have pretended to care, but I didn't.

***

When I was five, Mother took me to Davisville Public School to enrol me as a pupil in kindergarten. That's what all children in junior school were called in those days. I never understood why young kids must be called students. They certainly didn't study then. The teacher said we could all bring a teddy bear or a doll to school, so I brought Johnny. Most of the girls made faces at him because he was beginning to look quite shabby. Why on earth would I want a boy doll anyway, they said. But I didn't care. I continued to love Johnny even as his arms and, eventually, his legs fell off.

My brother and sister had already been through kindergarten; I found it very tedious. When I was asked to undo my shoelaces and then do them up, I rebelled, having done them up before going to school that morning. On one occasion, during rest period, which consisted of resting our heads on our arms and closing our eyes, one silly girl put her hand up and reported that I had my eyes open during rest period. I remember laughing and asking myself, *I wonder how she knew*. There were several other such incidents where I must have reported that I was bored, at which time the teacher, who lacked any humour, ordered me to go to the principal's office for the strap. I was genuinely shocked and replied, "I am too little and besides I am a girl." At that time corporal punishment was still all the rage, but girls were usually exempt. When I arrived at the principal's office, the principal looked surprised and escorted me to the nurse's office, where I stayed until it was time to go home.

There were other incidents related to my experiences at Cuthbert Crescent. One was when I was in kindergarten. I find it hard to admit to something that I am certainly not proud of, but I promised my friend

Mary Anne that I'd tell my story with all the warts. It happened shortly after we moved to Cuthbert Crescent. Mary knew that I was still suffering from the loss of my kitten. She found a stray tabby cat and brought it home for me to replace my beloved kitten. I took one look at the little cat and dropped it from the height of the garage roof. I was horrified with my act of cruelty and unable to look to see how it landed. Mary told me the small tabby managed somehow to run away and was never seen by us again. I do hope it found a kinder home.

There were a few rather unpleasant boys in our neighbourhood. One such boy lived almost across the street. He had a BB gun and, on one occasion, aimed it directly at me. I was very lucky because the BB barely missed my left eye, but I had a sore red welt for a few days on my cheekbone. The same boy, with a few of his friends, liked to torture well-brought-up boys, accusing them of being sissies. One day they grabbed Jimmy and took him into a garage where they started to hit his fingers to make them bleed. I was with a group of girls and bringing up the rear when I overheard the uproar and charged into the garage with a baseball bat that one of the older girls had been carrying. The nasty boys were so surprised, Jimmy and I made a quick exit before they could react.

In Grade 1, I had a lovely teacher called Miss Jarret. She was very nice to me, and I behaved very well, which pleased my parents. A boy that I liked, David Alexander, lived down the street. In the back garden of his family's house was an apple tree, and we often climbed it. One day when we were coming home from school, I spotted a stand of shiny B.C. apples at the front of Palumbo's grocery store on Yonge Street, around the corner from Carey Road. Without thinking very much, and with no one looking, I grabbed two off the shelf and ate one of them on my way home. When I got home, my father was just coming in from a tiring, unproductive day at his office. He asked me where I got the apple, and, flustered, I lied and said it was from David Alexander's apple tree. Father gave me one look. "That apple didn't come from David Alexander's tree." I confessed immediately, then, tired as he was, my dad took me by the arm and escorted me firmly the three blocks over to Yonge Street. When we entered Palumbo's grocery store, it was almost six o'clock. I had to confess my theft, return the one uneaten apple, and hand over my weekly allowance of five cents for the purchase of the apple I had eaten. I didn't understand why Mr. Palumbo was stifling a laugh. I never forget that lesson, and whenever I was tempted to steal an eraser or other item left carelessly by the owner, I refrained.

Behind a neighbour's house there was a hedge and behind the hedge was a shallow pit with a sandbox. Some of the younger kids used to congregate there to play either in the sandbox or with toy trucks. One boy, a little older than the rest of us, was somewhat precocious. He was also an exhibitionist. One day he announced that we should all take down our pants and display our private parts. I found this overwhelming, especially since he immediately pulled his shorts down to display his. In our family we all observed modesty, and my brother would have been shocked at such behaviour. However, I was not, particularly, and rather wanted to observe further but did not do so, realizing that that would mean that I would be obliged to display my intimate parts, which I certainly did not want to do.

There were two more memories I've never been able to erase from my mind. The first was of a harmless old man in a cart pulled by a rather bedraggled horse. He came by our street periodically, calling "Any old rags, bones, or bottles?" David and I tried to find a pail to fill with water for the horse. We were both upset when we heard other children shouting, "You killed Christ, old ragman." This was not Nazi Germany. This was Toronto "The Good," or was it? One other memory that affected me was the tragedy that happened to a family who lived a few doors away from our place. A young couple with one daughter was killed in an automobile accident, leaving their child an orphan. I liked the family, who had recently moved in and were so full of life and plans, and I especially liked the daughter, who was six years old, the same age as I was. Although I didn't witness the horrible accident, I felt devastated and often wondered afterward what had happened to my friend who was an orphan at such an early age.

Because Father didn't have work and there were three growing, energetic children, our parents decided it was time for us to have a summer holiday and to experience farm life. They heard of a farm on Lake Couchiching where there was a frame cottage near the water that the farmer would rent for very little money. So, the family moved there for a month. I loved it. There was a barn with a high haystack, horses, and cows. One day I found myself alone in the barnyard. There were a few hens and several very small yellow chicks. Suddenly, with no warning, I became a murderer. I picked up one little chick and threw it against the barn wall. I stopped in my tracks, turned, and left the barnyard without looking back. I had no idea why I did that.

The farm boys, ages about twelve and thirteen, allowed me to ride with them on the wagon. I was in seventh heaven. Almost every day I would climb aboard. I had two little cotton suits; one was a yellow patterned cotton that I wore for riding on the hay wagon, and one was an orange patterned cotton that I wore when I rode on the manure wagon. Other than that shocking incident, the summer holiday was a great success. All three of the Craig children were able to swim, even I (if not beautifully, with confidence).

The family had acquired a dog from our cousins. He came as a teenager in his dog years. He had an unfortunate name and by this time my parents felt it was too late to change it, so instead of just being called Gyp, Mother suggested that it was an abbreviated form of *Gypsophila* (baby's breath), so that became his formal name. But our dog was no sissy. He was a mixture of mastiff and German shepherd, and possibly other ingredients, and he was wonderful. He was gentle with us, and we were not gentle with him. He took the job as protector of the Craig children very much as if he were Nana from J. M. Barrie's *Peter Pan*. He escorted us everywhere he was allowed and never required a leash. While we were at the farm, Mother would walk Gyppy along the country road as she looked for wildflowers. There were six local border collie mixed-breed dogs who resented this newcomer and decided to gang up on him. They attacked him like a pack of wolves, and he simply grabbed the first one quite gently but firmly by the scruff of the neck and tossed it. He repeated the procedure with all the other dogs. The dogs never bothered him again and became quite friendly.

Mary and Sheila Craig visiting chicken coop in 1931.

Sister Mary, holding a doll, the author in a white bonnet and brother Jim.

Mary holding a Christmas tree, balanced on a sleigh pulled by Gyppy. (Photo by *Toronto Telegram*)

Chapter 3

When the end of our month at the cottage on the farm was up, we moved back to the city, not to Cuthbert Crescent but to Dawlish Avenue. It seems Father got a client and a job that paid, so we were back in Lawrence Park. Mary and I were enrolled at Blythwood Public School and Jimmy was enrolled in St. Paul's School for Boys on Deloraine Avenue. My Grade-1 teacher was nice to me, and I behaved impeccably, much to my mother's relief. The school was only a few years old, and everything was shiny. Set on the hill above Blythwood Road and the ravine, it stood out. Before it was built, I was told the pupils had to have classes in low-frame portables. The neighbourhood was growing, with pretty houses being built east of the school on Blythwood. But there was a marshy area on the north side, with Nanton's greenhouse and a creek where we would go to catch minnows and small turtles. Mother allowed this if there was a group and Gyppy accompanied us. One time I ventured too close and fell into the marsh. A nice, slightly older boy rescued me.

Later, Nanton's greenhouse was sold, and a developer managed to build on the site. Some years later one of the houses was for sale. It seems the owners were having trouble with a wet basement. I don't know if it was the same builder who managed to get a permit to destroy the pretty woods in which we loved to play, but I still remember with dismay when Mary and I, with three or four friends, tried in vain to save a beautiful huge beech tree. We formed a circle around it and linked hands. We kept this up for two days, but then when we left to go home, the tree was cut down. We were told it was in the way of a proposed subdivision. Even if I weren't the daughter of an architect, it horrified me and my friends to imagine something so magnificent destroyed. Why didn't the builder make it a feature by building a circular road around it and designing the houses in a concentric circle accordingly? The lack of imagination of the builder as well as the building department of the city hall was astounding.

***

Since Father's spare time was limited, and because his father had been a senior in the Masonic lodge, he decided that, rather than stay in the reserve army, he would join the Masons for continuity and enjoy men's company. When he came home from a meeting, I asked him about the evening. Although he told me very little, I gathered that they practised all sorts of secret rituals, which I found rather strange for grown men. I believe they did good works and helped the poor, but mainly they enjoyed the camaraderie of men.

***

The summer that I was eight, polio was prevalent, and it wasn't youngsters in the slums who were most likely to contract it, but rather children such as us, in middle-class districts where hands were frequently washed and food was sanitized. One of Jimmy's schoolmates at St. Paul's School for Boys contracted it and, on recovery, had a decided limp for the rest of his life. So, Mother and the three of us were shipped off for summer vacation to our cousins, who had an old, but big, cottage on Lake of Bays. Our cousins, the Cringans, were Bob, the eldest, Craig, Alex, Mary Evelyn, and Arthur.

That was about the time that our fellow Torontonians, doctors Banting and Best, discovered insulin; Mary Evelyn was diagnosed with type 1 diabetes at the age of seven, just in time to benefit from their discovery. Despite having to poke needles in her arms daily for many years, Mary Evelyn managed to bear two healthy sons and lived to be the oldest surviving diabetic in Canada, passing away at the age of ninety.

About the time of Mary Evelyn's diagnosis, I developed tonsilitis. It may sound hard to believe in today's world, but my tonsils and adenoids were removed at Dawlish Avenue, on the padded dining-room table, by the doctor who came to the house and with my father administering the gas anesthetic. This was not unusual at the time. Both Jimmy and Mary had had their tonsils removed on the kitchen table a few years before. I still remember being asked to inhale deeply and then waking up in bed with a sore throat.

Shortly after, I was offered ice cream and I felt very important and privileged, looking forward to bragging at school the next day.

Because Father had made a little money that year, he took the family for two weeks to Big Chief Lodge on Lake Couchiching. It had very tall and very beautiful trees, which I couldn't resist climbing. On one occasion I climbed up an extremely tall tree. I called down to my brother, "Look where I am," showing off, of course. Jimmy called our parents. When they saw me, they were horrified, but as calmly as he could, Father said, "Come down before you fall down." I took one look at the ground and froze. I realized that I was afraid to try to come down. Evidently the fire department wasn't that busy at the moment, so like a petrified kitten in a tree, I was rescued by two firemen who raised a tall ladder and brought me down. I was thoroughly embarrassed.

However, by the next fall, I seemed to have forgotten my lesson. One day I was with three friends from school and, feeling invincible, climbed the maple tree that hung over the mud sidewalk on the Dundurn side of our house. I wasn't content to simply climb the tree. I decided to try to leap from one branch to the other. That was a mistake. The next thing I remembered was waking up face down on the hard mud sidewalk. There was no one around. My friends had abandoned me, thinking that I was dead, I guess. There was very little traffic back then, and no one came by on the street, so as I came to, I was able to just lie there and ponder. Gradually, as my brain began to clear, I started to understand the basic rule of gravity. Then I picked myself up and crawled to the side door of the house, reached up, and rang the bell. Mother answered and looked at me with horror, since my face was covered with blood. But because it was 1938 and most Torontonians were still in the dark ages regarding modern medicine, especially neurology, she thought that, after carefully bandaging my face, all I would need was rest and I would be fine. Unfortunately, that wasn't the case.

Other than the bandages covering my nose, cheeks, and chin, I looked quite normal, but I started to have sharp pains down both arms, which I found odd since my arms were not affected by the fall. It wasn't until 1982, when I had a riding accident and my neck was x-rayed, that I was asked what happened to me when I was quite young to cause badly damaged cervical disks. When I told the doctor that I fell from a tree on my head when I was nine, he whistled and said how lucky I was that I wasn't older, or I might well have been a quadriplegic.

At the time of my fall, I had a very good friend who was not with us when I fell from the tree. I don't believe she would have deserted me. Her name was Sheila Knox. She lived three blocks north of Dawlish and she used to call for me on the way to school. Then we would wrestle most of the way until we were in view of the school, when we started to walk like the other girls. We both had black braids, and if any of the boys tried to pull them, they would regret it. We were friendly with most of the girls and mixed in with several of the boys also. But there were half a dozen or more boys at school who behaved as if they were superior to the girls. They called us dames. They were not referring to us as if we had the order of knighthood; the term was used in a derogatory sense. The only way we could prove ourselves to these young bullies-in-training was to defeat them in their own game, which was by physical prowess. We engaged them in wrestling matches.

They also considered themselves superior to the family of a caretaker who lived on Mount Pleasant Road. I remind my readers that this was the time of the Depression. One day we overheard them planning to gang up on the five sons of the caretaker and to beat them up after school on their way home. Sheila and I were incensed and not only warned the eldest boy, but also decided to join them in the fight. We had the advantage of surprise. It wasn't easy, but we managed to win the battle and, for a time, they stopped taunting us.

I was invited to Sheila's tenth birthday party, which consisted of boys and girls she knew from church. When we all stood around the birthday table just before sitting down, an adult started a prayer. I fumbled and didn't know what to do when everyone else made the sign of the cross. A boy said, "I see you're not a Catholic," and I had to admit I was not, but I was embarrassed at not knowing the routine, and for the first time in my Protestant community, I felt like an outsider. The prayer of thanks was to God, and their god and mine were the same, after all. I think other than the Connellys, an Irish Catholic family with one small son, Tommy, who lived immediately to the south of us, the Barretts, whose backyard abutted the southwest corner of ours, and Steve and Mary McGrath, a childless couple who lived next door to us, the Knox Family were, to the best of my knowledge, the only Catholics in Protestant Lawrence Park.

Helen Barrett (aka Tony), who in adulthood became my friend, confided in me that of all the mothers in Lawrence Park, my mother was the only one who invited her and her brother and sister into her house. Steve and Mary McGrath didn't seem to go to church, but were very friendly with me, and I quite loved Mary, a pretty woman probably in her forties, whom I used to visit.

Steve used to play the horses, and one day he got lucky and made a small fortune. After that, instead of enjoying their main floor living room, they started entertaining their friends in their recreation room in the basement. I overheard Father commenting to Mother that the calibre of the McGraths' friends had changed, and not for the better. It seems that with the sudden fortune, that nice couple started to drink in excess, and that must have caused the change in their choice of friends.

After a while, I noticed that Mary's health had deteriorated, and she started walking with a cane and spending a lot of time in her bedroom, where I visited her. One day sometime later, a black car arrived at their front door and two men in black suits carried a stretcher. A short time later, they left with their burden completely covered with a white sheet, my first adult friend, Mary. A few days later, a hearse arrived. I asked my parents to allow me to see her before she was taken to Blessed Sacrament Church for her funeral. Pink was her favourite colour, so I cut a lovely pink rose from our garden and placed it in Mary's hand, which was the colour of porcelain. She was displayed in her coffin in the living room, wearing a soft grey dress with her hair freshly done. This was my first experience of death. It was sad but gentle.

Unfortunately, Steve started drinking more and more; he had a lady friend who was his drinking partner move in and, eventually, they were married. They used to invite me in, but I didn't need my parents to tell me to stay clear of their basement, although I must admit I was somewhat fascinated by the rough types that frequented it, including one who turned out to be Steve's bootlegger. Occasionally I still visited when my parents weren't home, but soon the excitement of being accepted by this very different group from those I was brought up with, and being offered as much ginger ale as I could drink, wore off and I didn't visit anymore.

***

When winter came that year, it was time to go skating with my sister, Mary, and her friends. At the Yonge Street–end of our street was the start of the ravine. It had a well-maintained ice-skating rink in a park-like setting that we approached by steps from Dawlish. Before setting off, carrying my skates over my shoulder, I ate two rather green apples. It was a very cold day with a north wind. Frankly, I never did enjoy skating, and Mary's hand-me-down figure skates didn't feel comfortable. First, my feet got cold and then I started to get pain in my lower extremities. The pain got worse, and I felt I would cry. Finally, it was too much, and I almost begged Mary and her friend to help me off with the skates and help me home, which they did, albeit grudgingly.

When we got home, Mother and Father were off visiting friends and only Pearl Apostle, our maid, a lively farm girl from Saskatchewan with few social graces, was there. She told me to go upstairs to bed. Mary and Jimmy told me I was a sissy. I waited for my mommy, quietly sobbing in bed.

When my parents came home, they took my situation quite seriously and, after a short time, phoned Dr. Park, our family doctor who lived just four blocks away. He came over and immediately contacted another doctor, who also came to our house. After inspecting me, the two doctors had a short conversation with my parents and then phoned the hospital to check if the OR was available for that night. I didn't understand what was going on but found out later that they determined I had acute appendicitis. I heard animated conversation, and the next thing I knew, I was bundled up.

Driven by Father, accompanied by Mother, we drove to a very intimidating large Victorian building at the corner of College and Elizabeth streets. This turned out to be the Hospital for Sick Children. I was taken to a room with one other very young sick girl, and when we arrived, the nurse put a curtain around her bed. I remember being embarrassed as the nurse removed all my clothes, including my underpants, without even asking permission. She then put a short cotton nightshirt on me, and I was wheeled on a high bed to a very bright room where a male orderly lifted me to an operating table. I asked if I should open my mouth because that was what I was asked to do at my tonsil operation not that long before. This caused a slight stir and an odd chuckle. Shortly, a doctor put a mask on my face. I was asked to breathe deeply and then I knew nothing until I woke up in my room alone. The sick roommate was gone when I woke up. I think she must have died.

The original Toronto Children's Hospital.

I spent five days in bed in the hospital, and I was not allowed to move. That was a far cry from today, when I would have been encouraged to move soon after surgery and sent home the next day.

At home, I was greeted by Mary and Jimmy, who were nicer to me than before, and by Pearl, who came into the bedroom where Mary and I were talking. After a short pause, she asked if either of us had started to bleed yet. We looked at one another in shock, not knowing what she was talking about. Then she said sorry, of course, you're too young. That was the era when some mothers were too shy to discuss such things as menstruation with their daughters.

***

It was October, and for the first time, the Craig children were allowed to go out on Halloween unaccompanied by their dad. I was told to stay close to my sister and brother. Mary looked lovely dressed up as a pirate princess. Jimmy was a dashing pirate, and I found a pair of Jimmy's old breeches in the attic, knee socks, and a pair of his old shoes, which miraculously fitted me. So, I too went as a pirate, complete with an eye patch. I felt quite indomitable in boys' clothes and rather entitled. A couple of schoolmates joined us.

As soon as I could, I found some older boys of about twelve and thought that now was the perfect chance to tease them, which I did. Suddenly I was alone with three of them when one of them said, "Let's give this little brat a beating that he won't forget for quite a while." That's when I got frightened and as they got near me, I blurted out, "I'm a girl." They stopped dead in their tracks, and one of them said, "Then behave like one," and they stamped off.

I found Jimmy and Mary and, feeling thoroughly chastised, was soon glad to go home, thinking all the time that perhaps it wasn't all roses being a boy after all. Somehow my desire to wrestle and defeat boys was not as much fun as before. One of my protagonists, a bit of a bully, accosted me in the schoolyard, and although I didn't put up much of a fight, he pushed me hard and my head cracked against the concrete. I vowed then and there never again to wrestle with a boy. They were altogether too strong. I kept my vow.

Chapter 4

In the spring of 1939, my father was particularly vocal in his disgust for the German dictator Adolf Hitler. Shortly after that, my parents were delighted to hear that King George VI and Queen Elizabeth, with their two daughters, were to make a state visit to Canada. They were to pass through Toronto and make a stop at the then-North Toronto railway station with its marble interior and clock tower. Now it is Toronto's most impressive LCBO. Dad had a close friend who owned a small monument factory situated about sixty feet south of the station, and he arranged for our family to stand with him on the roof, to be parallel with the royal family as they disembarked from their train and waved at us and the crowds below.

Princess Elizabeth was born in April 1926, the same month and year as Jimmy. Her sister, Margaret, was slightly younger than I was. It seems that the royal family had planned to land in Halifax on a battleship but were informed that war with Germany seemed to be inevitable and, if so, the battleship would be needed, so they travelled by steamship instead. I rather suspect that the British war office was worried for the royal family's safety and wanted them away from any war zone.

Two short years later, our family would once again stand to wave as a train pulled out of that station, but this time it would be our father leaving for Halifax to board a ship for England. Canada had declared a war against Germany a few days after Britain in September of 1939.

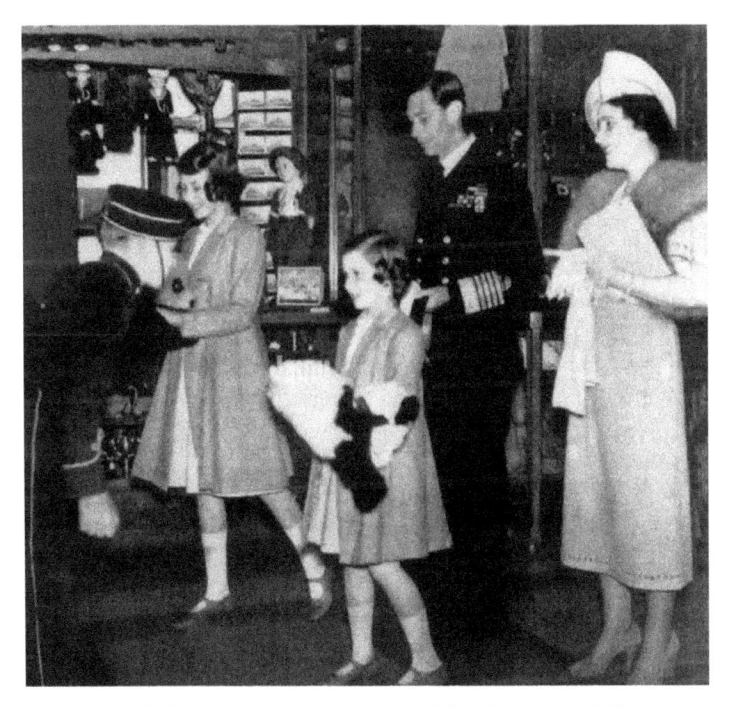

The Royal Couple with Princess Elizabeth and Princess Margaret arriving at the Royal York Hotel.

***

When I was ten, I joined the Girl Guides. Mary had joined earlier. We each came home with boxes of Girl Guide cookies, which we were to sell for charity. On the cover of each box was printed "Be Prepared" (the Girl Guides' motto.) Father chuckled and asked what would happen to him if he ate a cookie.

Although my eleventh birthday was still a while away, and I was painfully aware that both Jimmy and Mary had to wait for their respective thirteenth birthdays to get a bicycle, I was longing to have the freedom that a bike would allow me. Accordingly, I made a proposition to my parents. I was told that a new bike, even on sale, would cost thirty dollars I also knew that I would get ten cents each time I cut the lawn and ten cents if I did the dishes all by myself. The same would go for raking leaves and shovelling the snow. I asked if they would consider a bike for my eleventh birthday if I saved almost all of the cost. I pointed out that my eleventh birthday was still a while away, and I was bound to earn the money somehow. Thinking that it was a good thing for their overactive daughter to have a goal and use up some of her overabundant energy, they checked with Mary and Jimmy, who thought it was a great idea since I would do chores that they wouldn't have to do and that would make me less disruptive. So they agreed.

When my eleventh birthday arrived, I was still short six dollars of my goal and was thrilled despite that to find a brand-new red bicycle awaiting me when I came down for breakfast on May 14, 1940. With my red bicycle, I was very mobile and thoroughly enjoyed the freedom it offered.

I had been in the Girl Guides for a year and was enjoying the camaraderie of girls who also enjoyed the outdoors, being part of a team, and getting things done. It was very exciting to be told that I was now to become a patrol leader. My patrol and I decided that we would excel, and we did, helping people with disabilities across the street and helping out with all sorts of volunteer work with those less fortunate, including young mothers whose husbands had joined the armed services. We were especially good at learning outdoor skills. We also were the top group in our area for sales of Girl Guide cookies.

Unfortunately, I was not very good at controlling my naughty streak. Our meetings took place in the Blythwood School gym on Friday evenings. Before leaving one Friday, I decided to give the group a laugh and drew a chalk caricature of the school principal, Mr. Follis, on the blackboard. I accentuated his rather comical farmer's haircut and printed Mr. Fossil under the drawing. We all enjoyed a quick laugh, but then the caretaker dimmed the lights, and we all made a quick exit. By the time I realized that I had forgotten to wipe the drawing off the board, it was too late to go back.

Monday morning came and Mr. Follis announced that all of the Grade 7 and 8 classes were to file through the gym. He was there to question each one as to whether or not he or she could point out the culprit who had done a rude chalk drawing (which, mercifully, had been removed). My Grade 7 class were each asked and not one of us said a word. Then the Grade 8 class assembled, and one of the boys who didn't like me announced that I was the guilty party.

Mr. Follis wasn't sure what punishment I was to receive. He couldn't very well fail me because my marks were too high. So he attempted to have me thrown out of Girl Guides, and this also didn't work. In September, I was in Grade 8.

My beloved Grade-7 teacher, Mr. Freestone, had told me at the end of the Grade-7 year that I had a talent for the stage and should pursue it in some form. When the fall of 1941 arrived, and the war in Europe was not going well for the Allies, he invited me to read the wonderful poem by the Canadian poet and physician Lieutenant-Colonel John McCrae "In Flanders Fields" and to recite it on November 11, Remembrance Day. As I waited for my turn in the school auditorium, I realized that I was being passed over when the principal Mr. Follis introduced a boy reading some other poem as the final item on the agenda. I knew then the folly of antagonizing someone who had total control of the situation.

Now school was finishing for the year and there was another threat of polio. My parents quickly looked for a summer retreat for the whole family. Father decided to take a well-deserved break and figured he could work out of the city on designs and take the family far away from the city.

A friend of Dad's told him of a cottage available for rent in Go Home Bay, a small rocky area on the east coast of Georgian Bay. It had to be accessed by boat, and the closest approach was from Midland, some fifteen miles south. There were two large seaworthy ferry boats that could handle the wild waters of the Georgian Bay. So, the Craig family, including Gypsophila, set out for Midland in their merry Oldsmobile, recently purchased by Dad in

Southampton, where he was building a school. We all loved it, but it was green, and I would have preferred red.

When we got to Midland and boarded the SS *Midland City*, I was very excited. I'd never seen anything quite so thrilling. Instead of grass and trees, there was deep rolling water with nothing on the horizon but small, almost uninhabited islands with the occasional cottage set high up. Georgian Bay was not like anything else I had ever seen. Father explained that about ninety miles north of Toronto the farmland ceases to exist and instead of deciduous trees, which shed their leaves, various varieties of the pine family take over. Everywhere I looked were rounded, rocky islands, many of them shades of pink and dark red juxtaposed against dark rocks that looked, to me, like whales. I instantly fell in love with this new world. Father explained that this rock formation was one of the oldest in the world. It is called the Precambrian Shield and stretches to Scandinavia and Siberia. The pine trees were not straight but seemed to be leaning toward the east, due to the strong prevailing winds from the west.

The trip from Midland to Go Home Bay was fairly smooth that first time, but I was told it wasn't always the case. When we arrived at Go Home Bay, the ship had to navigate two rather narrow passages until it pulled up at Government Dock and we disembarked. From there we took a water taxi back a short distance to the cottage where we would spend the summer. The modest cottage was framed and stained dark brown and was situated above a rocky cliff with a sheer drop of about thirty feet to the water below.

We always knew when the SS *Midland City* was arriving because almost half an hour before her arrival, we started to hear the beat of her motor and we could feel it under our feet, and sure enough, shortly we could see her coming around the bend toward our narrow channel.

Amenities there were almost none. I loved it. There was an outhouse in the place of a toilet, there was a hand pump to bring the water up from and to the lake, and an icehouse where blocks of ice were stored in sawdust. They were cut from the lake ice in the early spring and, as needed, brought from the icehouse to the simple kitchen and placed in the icebox over the shelf where milk, meat, fish, eggs, and other perishables were kept. There was, of course, no hydroelectric power. But there were coal oil lamps and even Aladdin lamps with delicate chimneys. As for boats, there were only two, a canoe and a rowboat. There was a nine-horsepower motor but, at first, only Father used it. The rest of us had to row.

All food and supplies were delivered by boat, which came by once a week with orders from the week before. Mother was in seventh heaven with views of our island. Mother had always painted and had a natural talent. Georgian Bay, the favourite of the Group of Seven, was also a favourite of Mother's. She would sit for hours on a rock with her sketch box and oil paints and draw and paint those rocky shores in the distance surrounded by clear water.

Also a favourite of Mother's to paint was a lily pond nestled between large rocks bordering the west side of the island. But Mother insisted on being accompanied by Gyppy when she painted. She wasn't worried about bears, although occasionally one would be sighted, but she was very nervous about the possibility of a snake slithering past her ankle, and she had reason to worry because there was an unwelcome snake that none of us wanted to encounter and whose habitat was rocky Georgian Bay. That was the massasauga rattlesnake. Although shy, this snake, if threatened, would lift its tail, which had a rattle for each year of its life, and first rattle as a warning. If the rattle was unheeded, it would then strike. The adult snake is not usually much more than thirty inches or so in length, but it is not attractive in appearance (I know because I've encountered a few in my time). Its bite is not deadly if antivenom is administered soon, but it can be if not. But I don't want to scare any reader away. There is not much likelihood of running into a rattlesnake these days. But if you do, heed its warning.

What we did have, and which we still do, in eastern Georgian Bay is the rather beautiful fox snake. In rare cases, it can grow up to eight feet in length and has a slender body with gold and rich brown markings and a quizzical face set in a friendly shrimp-coloured head. It is gentle and won't bite.

***

Go Home Bay was founded by a group of University of Toronto professors and graduates who delighted in the rugged beauty of the area. They made it part of their mandate that only graduates of the university would be allowed to buy in or rent in Go Home Bay. Fortunately, Father was a grad. The reader can observe that wealth was not a factor, but I can't help but comment on the fact that many of our public leaders spent at least part of their youth summering in Go Home Bay.

My dad liked to fish and insisted on teaching each of his children how to kill and clean the catch. I wasn't keen on baiting the hook because I didn't like putting the hook through the worm and seeing it wriggle in pain. Mother didn't either, but she had a natural knack for fishing and caught the largest pickerel. We three kids became quite proficient in the rough water of Georgian Bay and also learned some camping tricks from the local Métis that even teenagers at camp don't usually learn. Altogether that summer was a great success. But then it was time to go back to school.

Chapter 5

I had just reached puberty earlier than my older sister and was distressed that never before had I felt so itchy and miserable. Every part of my body seemed to be affected. When I touched my arm, it seemed to break out in a rash, and the worst part was yet to come. After the rash came weeks of intense pain, it seems from every nerve ending. I had had a particularly severe case of chicken pox as a small child, which was probably the underlying cause. It was never diagnosed by Dr. Park, who decided it was a severe case of hives. But what happened then was something that I firmly believe was shingles. And to this day I keep my Shingrix vaccination up to date.

After that, I started to gain weight, although I was not eating more. I lost my energy. My face began to thicken, my eyes got puffy, and my hair started to get frizzy. My parents, being conscientious people, had sent me to the doctor that most parents in Lawrence Park usually sent their children to. This was Dr. Alan Brown, a pediatrician.

When I arrived in his office, the good doctor examined me. I was very shy and hated the way I looked. The 1939–1945 war was already in its second year, and the good doctor looked me up and down and said, "If the Germans could see your backside, they'd run a mile." Dr. Brown was rather overweight himself, and mortified as I was, I managed to look him up and down and blurt out, "Is that so?"

Dr. Brown was also known to a friend of mine, Donald Teskey, who later became my dentist. Young Donald was shy and unsure of himself. When he first was sent to Dr. Brown, the good doctor asked him mockingly why he didn't bring his knitting. Despite his lack of bedside manner, Dr. Brown was probably a good diagnostician. He pronounced that I had hypothyroidism. He then prescribed a form of thyroid treatment that was in a fairly primitive state back then, and I've been told by my niece, Alison, who seems to be knowledgeable about all things medical, that the treatment contained steroids. Now this treatment may have stunted my growth but not my enthusiasm for adventure and a constant desire to try new things.

There was no point in feeling sorry for myself because of my unattractive appearance. One of my friends suggested I have a new nickname, so it was decided it should be the opposite of what I was. We chose "Dainty."

At that time, playing with marbles was a popular activity among preteens. In late March and April, with most of the snow and ice gone, we eleven- and twelve-year-olds would play on the road with marbles, shooting at each other. If one hit another, then the shooter added that to their take. I asked Jimmy to cut me an eight-inch-high by sixteen-inch-wide board with small holes for marbles. I then added black semicircles above the holes. "Dainty's Shooting Alley" was printed at the top half and the rest was in bright colours. This attracted many of the children, and I won far too many marbles. I became embarrassed and decided to either cut the holes larger or retire "Dainty's Shooting Alley," which I did.

My early Grade-8 year at Blythwood School was, for the most part, traumatic. I didn't enjoy the transition from carefree childhood to puberty. I no longer wanted to enjoy sports and fool around with my earlier pal Sheila Knox. I spent more time with classmates who lived nearby. I took piano lessons from a very nice lady who lived a few blocks away and seemed to think I had a natural talent. But I wasn't interested in improving my skills if it meant endlessly practising scales or learning new pieces on the piano. I'm afraid I was a disappointment to my parents, who always meant the best for their children. I did pass my Grade-8 piano and decided to continue, but my teacher gave a recital and asked me to open it with "God Save the King," which I knew by heart, and it was easy. But as I started to play the first bar, my father in uniform stood up, and I froze and couldn't continue even when someone handed me the music.

By this time Jim was in his second year of high school at UTS (University of Toronto Schools). Mary was in her first year of high school at Lawrence Park Collegiate, and Father was soon to be shipped overseas.

When, finally, my health was no longer an issue, I settled in for a final term at Blythwood School. My classmates were all at least twelve years old. Some were already teenagers. I was still overweight but accepted a new stage in my life. I was enjoying Grade 8. Toward the end of the school year, some of the classes were told that they were recommended for high school and wouldn't have to write the entrance exam.

I was one of these groups, and since we had no more schoolwork, we decided to put on a play. I was cast as Miss Pinkerton, a forty-three-year-old pretending to be twenty-three. As an admirer of ZaSu Pitts, a Hollywood comedienne, I modelled my character after her. My second attempt at acting was more successful than my first as a dormouse in *Alice Through the Looking Glass*. My classmates started calling me Pinky. Mr. Follis was no longer angry with me and smiled when he handed me my silver medal, which read "Eight years good conduct, regularity and diligence," and, in fact, it isn't silver but metal. I still have it somewhere in a drawer.

At this time, I noticed that Father seemed excited and a bit on edge. I asked Mother what was causing our dad's strange behaviour. It seems Craig and Madill had passed almost all the hurdles architectural firms have to pass on their way to achieving a much-sought-after assignment. This was to design the veteran's hospital in Sunnybrook Park. Almost at the last hour, the job was awarded instead to John C. Parkin. The war was by now in its second year, and it didn't look promising for the Allies. Father was an old soldier and a loyal Canadian. I expect that instead of joining the Masons, he regretted the fact that he had not stayed in the army reserve after the Great War. Men who had been officers overseas were used to men's company and some stayed on in the militia and rose in rank with time. When the 1939 war broke out, his friend Wilf Curtis had the rank of air vice-marshal, and other officers he had served with in the Great War, as it was called, were brigadiers.

However, he decided rank wasn't important and perhaps he should offer his services to his country. He discussed it with my mother, who told him he and he alone had to decide what to do. So, he went to the depot and volunteered. At this time, the Canadian army overseas was entirely composed of volunteers. He passed his physical A-1. From there he received his first war rank of major and was immediately dispatched to Newmarket for basic training.

The only contact we had with him was once every week, usually after the camp's church parade, when Mother would drive the shiny 1939 Oldsmobile with Jimmy in the front and Gyppy, Mary, and me in the back. We always took the backroads to Newmarket; there was no direct route and, weather permitting, we would have a picnic en route beside a farmer's field. Our visits were not very long because there was strict discipline in the camp, and Gyppy had to be on leash the whole time.

All the Craig children had attended Sunday school since we were five years old, and now church had taken over. The family attended St. George's United Church on Duplex Avenue. I found the minister an affable man. It turned out he was also a pacifist. One Sunday we were all in the family pew in the third row when the minister, speaking of war and soldiers and looking straight at us, made the comment, "They think they are right, but they are misguided," at which point Father rose immediately, followed by Mother and the three Craig children, and walked down the aisle, never to enter that church again.

***

Mother still bristled inwardly at having been refused entry to the school of architecture at the age of twenty-two because, as she was told, "the men would never accept a girl." Mother knew that the girls at her old school, Branksome Hall, had all the rights of the boys at UTS and that they had a debating society and, if qualified, could participate in all the sports offered at the school. She also knew that it would be impossible to enrol her two daughters at Branksome on the income of a major, even subsidized by his savings from his architecture earnings the few years before. Mother had a bold plan. She knew that Edith M. Read, the principal, was a feminist and would understand Mother's overwhelming desire to give her daughters the same advantage as her son. Miss Read was aware of Mother's prowess at the school, that she had been a gold medalist and head girl, and that she was a patriot. So, Miss Read would accept both Mary and me for the price of one of us. Mother leapt at the opportunity, determined to budget accordingly.

Summer arrived and instead of going to summer camp, which most of our classmates did, Mary and I went to summer school at Branksome Hall, which cost a great deal less and which we thoroughly enjoyed. It seems that Bishop Strachan School for girls in Toronto had offered to take some of the staff and all the girls enrolled in a prestigious English girl's school named Sherborne School for the duration of the war for safety. When the Sherborne contingent was already on a ship headed for Halifax, the Bishop Strachan School wasn't expecting them so soon and said they were not ready to receive them. That was when our indomitable principal, Edith M. Read, having just heard the news, immediately offered to house all of them in what is now named Sherborne House. Her offer was accepted, and the girls arrived, escorted by a young woman teacher who was only twenty-eight years old. She was tall and slender, with short, dark, wavy hair, and with a handsome, intelligent face. Her name was Dana Reader-Harris. She invited us to join her summer English class, and we were given an assignment to write a short poem that would express our feelings when in different environments.

I sent "Contrasts" to Father, who had just arrived in England. He kept it and asked me to keep it as well, so here it is.

CONTRASTS
By: Sheila Craig

My heart's in the Northland
Where bitter winds blow
Where the rocks are washed clean
And crooked pines grow.

The waves tipped with white caps
crash loud on the shore,
while the gulls add their squawk
to the thundering roar.

In the lee of the rocks the lily pond lies,
where frogs sit on lily pads,
blinking their eyes
The arrows wild orchids
and ferns growing there
mid the deep purple shadows
make a picture so rare.
the clanging of the street cars
the smell of gasoline,
the noise of yelling paper boys,
The crowds that surge between
the buildings in the narrow streets
beneath the thick smokescreen
make me wish I were up north again
where the winds blow fresh and clean.

Sheila Craig Waengler 57

Georgian Bay—exciting lively blue water with a rocky shoreline.

Lily Pond, which mother often included in her sketches of Georgian Bay. When she drew, Gyppy would sit sentinel, protecting her from snakes or other predators.

We Canadian girls were in the minority. The Sherborne School girls settled in and enjoyed Branksome's athletic facilities, which were minimal according to today's standards. There was no homework, and we could utilize all the sports facilities including the tennis courts, the volleyball courts, and basketball courts.

My Grade-9 classroom was on the ground floor of Scott House, named after Miss Scott, not only a former principal of Branksome, but also a former teacher at Grandmother's school, Ottawa Ladies' College. Scott House bordered a tennis court on the south side and Rosedale Presbyterian Church on the north, which is situated at the southeast corner of South Drive and what then was called Huntley Street (now Mount Pleasant Road). The church still stands, but little Scott House was demolished long ago to make way for Branksome's expansion and modernization. I have many happy memories of that small house.

The first day of school I looked around at my new classmates, who almost all looked very much at home in their school uniforms. The majority of the girls were slender with straight hair, either brown or blond. I had my black pigtails, was still overweight, and felt out of place. There was one girl who also looked out of place. She had frizzy hair loosely tied in two semi-pigtails. When she walked, she toed out (a sign of flat feet), but her face was full of life. We looked at one another and immediately started laughing. For the next five years, we were close friends and the friendship remained intact. Whereas my first good friend also didn't fit into the mold by being Catholic in a sea of Protestants, my new friend, Judy Godfrey, was also of a rarity in that she was Jewish in a school of probably 95 percent Protestants.

Scott House, with our Grade 9 classroom at Branksome Hall.

Neither of us was very good at sports, but we were enthusiastic and very energetic. When I played softball and was up at bat, I often hit a foul ball or struck out. But when I connected with the ball, it could have gone straight over Scott House, and it was almost always a home run. In basketball, I would have been a great guard, but unfortunately, guards must be tall, and I was just five foot four. Mary was good at basketball and, although almost five foot six, a bit short for guard, it didn't matter because she played forward and made the team.

Judy and I decided that since we believed we had talent as performers and abundant energy and wanted to be part of the sports action, we must create something. So, we became self-appointed cheerleaders. I asked our

Scottish bagpipe player, Pipe Major Fraser, who performed at all school formal functions, to translate our cheer to Gaelic, which I felt was suitable for a school that wore a kilt and had Scottish traditions. He obliged.

We also thought we needed a nickname and, looking at one another, we decided to name ourselves. And since we found ourselves anything but beautiful, we would call ourselves Love and Love. But to differentiate one another we would be Love 1 and Love 2. I suggested that Judy should be Love 1 on her birthday and I would take over as Love 1 on my birthday, two months later Judy wasn't entirely happy with this arrangement but was obliging.

Love 1 in summer uniform and Love 2 at Branksome.

Mother with Jimmy, Mary, and Sheila, posing on the terrace at 123 Dawlish.

Chapter 6

Judy played the piano and could read music without difficulty. Unfortunately, I did not, although I continued to take piano lessons and enjoyed playing Bach and Beethoven in particular. Many of our daytime classmates, who brought sandwiches to school for lunch, spent their time before going back to classes either sitting cross-legged on the grass in good weather and playing bridge or, in the fall and winter, in the library, also playing bridge. Judy and I were not interested in such sedentary activity. We liked to keep moving, and we discovered we could harmonize to almost any tune. We built up a repertoire with three or four favourites. So, we would go to one bridge group and then move on to the next, who sometimes requested a particular number.

After a while, we decided to include the front hall and the entrance to the staff room, since we thought we were getting rather good. This latest effort was received with mixed response. There were three or four teachers who found us rather amusing and enjoyed a laugh in the middle of the school routine, but there was also some staff who were not even slightly amused by our antics. And then there was Ainsley McMichael, a formidable figure, tall and very large. She was Miss Read's assistant in her office. I can still picture the two of them walking side by side, huge Ainsley and tiny, slender but powerful Edith M. Read. We took care to make ourselves scarce if the principal was anywhere nearby, and if we passed Ainsley McMichael's office, we always moved very quickly, because she would give us each a smack on our derrière if she could catch us going past her door. Our behaviour and that Ainsley McMichael would never be tolerated in today's world.

When our class was to choose two representatives to perform at a senior school recital with a combination of dance and music, Dianna Windeyer was chosen to do a fancy tap dance, and Love and I were quite delighted to be allowed to perform the Angel and the Devil while doing a tap dance that we created ourselves.

I considered leaving out the balance of Judy's and my silly antics while at Branksome Hall back in the 1940s, while much of the world was suffering and dying during that dreadful six-year war. Still, Judy, aka Love 2, told me she would be very put out if I didn't include at least some of our antics.

One long weekend, Mother allowed Mary and me to stay over at Ruth (aka Pickle) Harris's house. Her father was a widower and a barrister who worked long hours, and Pickle was looked after by his very efficient housekeeper. Mr. Harris was delighted to hear that his daughter, whom he felt was deprived in some way, wanted to have three of her schoolmates to stay for the weekend when he would be out of town on a case. Pickle invited her classmate, my sister Mary, as well as Judy (Love 2) and me.

    We all explored the basement and found a machine that was used in the old days to make ice cream. Pickle was somewhat foggy about the whole procedure, which involved salt as a hardener and, of course, cream and sugar as well as flavouring. It required lots of hard work to churn the substance. Finally, we had ice cream, but when we tasted it, it was very salty. It seems there was a small leak. Well, after all our hard work, we wanted a solution. The next-door neighbour, Arthur Meighen, was at home, and Pickle and I knocked on his door. Pickle assumed that, because he was knowledgeable about the world and domestic affairs, as a distinguished lawyer as well as a former Prime Minister of Canada now enjoying retirement in the mid-sixties, he would know how to get rid of the salt from our ice cream. He smiled and for want of any solution other than repairing the hole and starting again, he just suggested that we add more sugar. Regrettably, we didn't have homemade ice cream for dinner.

    Love and I asked if we could explore the attic because Pickle's older brother, who was by then in the armed forces and away at war, had a trunk of old clothes and costumes in the attic. We found two sets of red flannel underwear. By tucking up the legs and arms, we were each able to wear a set. Then the two of us decided we would wait until after midnight and then go to the school, climb in a basement window, find chalk, and draw a sign in the middle of the intersection of Huntley Street and Elm Avenue.

We couldn't find an unlocked window at the main school, so went to Sherborne House, where we found the basement window unlocked and a classroom with a stash of chalk. Sherborne House is on the southwest corner of Elm Avenue and Mount Pleasant Road (at the time, sleepy little Huntley Street). So, we took our chalk to the middle of the road and, after two trips to replenish the chalk and an hour's work, we had a four-foot-high sign that read "WE LOVE PLAUNT." Jean Plaunt was the head girl, about five foot nine and a terrific athlete, and we found her quite wonderful. Neither Judy nor I had had anything much to do with boys at this time, but like most other adolescents, we found it necessary to hero worship some attractive slightly older individual who, because it was an all-girls school, was a female.

We rested and waited. But after all the efforts, no cars or people came by. We were disappointed and a little tired by this time. Finally, a car appeared. The occupants were two open-jawed policemen. After much shaking of their heads, they simply told us to go home and go to bed.

But of course, that wasn't the end of the nonsense. I had always been fascinated with the university campus, and Love and I decided to visit it, specifically the medical building. When the next long weekend arrived, we took ourselves down to U of T, having found a diagram that showed the layout of the campus. We found the medical building, and, to our delight, we once again found an unlocked basement window. How times have changed since 1942. Perhaps I'm wrong, but it seems there were no campus police, and no one seemed worried about the possibility of theft or vandalism. Once in the building, we were almost immediately confronted by a skeleton. Then we knew we had found the right place. We decided to name this very real individual, and after a short discussion, we chose the name Cherubim Sweetness, a neutral name, since we couldn't determine whether the skeleton was male or female. Then we moved to another room that had large containers. When we opened the lid and pulled out the drawer of one container, there was a very strong aroma that we determined was formaldehyde. Inside were several wrapped items that were parts of human beings. At this point, we decided we had enough and climbed back the way we'd come in. We were quite relieved that we had not been discovered. I suddenly had a feeling that I had trodden on sacred ground where I had no business being.

I will end this chapter with one more episode of Love and Love's silly adventures. This one could have ended badly. I believe it was our over-the-top ridiculous behaviour that saved the day. It was a Saturday, and Mary and two of her classmates, as well as Love and I with Gyppy, were starting to walk toward Sunnybrook Park. The end of Dawlish Avenue is interrupted by a little wood and a street called Pinedale, which runs downhill. At the top of the hill, there was a moving van, the rear door open with a ramp. An upright piano had just been mounted into the van. I challenged Love to climb in and play something on the piano. She rather reluctantly did, and I climbed in as well. Just as she was about to play, the driver and his assistant came out of the house. We decided to hide rather than be discovered.

Suddenly the ramp was pushed in and the door was slammed shut. We could hear our friends shouting, "Bye Loves," and Gyppy barking as the truck backed up. What to do? We decided to do nothing for the moment since we assumed the driver would deliver the piano somewhere in Toronto. But shortly, we realized that this was not the case because the van had picked up speed and was driving on a highway. After a while, we realized that this might be a much longer trip than we initially thought, so it was decided that Love should start playing the piano and we would both sing. That way we would be discovered before we were too far out in the country.

Shortly, the van pulled over to the side. The rear door was rolled open, and two burly men appeared. Immediately they invited us to join them in the cab, where I sat beside the driver, Love sat beside me, and the other man sat next to Love, by the door. They explained that the piano was to go to a farm of a friend, which was where we were heading.

In 1942 slacks were still not worn by girls. We were in our regular weekend attire, which was a skirt and knee socks. Shortly, Love started to get agitated, and I realized that she was having trouble with the man beside her. Fortunately, we arrived at the farm shortly thereafter. Love whispered to me, saying that the man beside her had wandering hands and would I like to change places. I'm afraid I turned her down. But then, as soon as the piano was moved to the parlour of the farm, the two invited us for an inspection of their friend's property. Also, the driver was to feed the chickens and to check on the pigs. First, he showed us the chicken coop and distributed the seeds as well as checked for eggs, which were to go in the refrigerator. Then we went to visit the pigpen. At this point, both movers started to get amorous. I still remember the scene, Love and I were running around the pigpen with the two of them in pursuit.

I ran to the screen door that opened into the parlour. We headed for the piano with me shouting to Love to play "Jamboree Jones," which she did. I started dancing back and forth while both of us did a lively performance of that college song. The movers were stymied by our behaviour. When we stopped for breath, I announced in as definite a voice as I could that one of our three friends with us at the house in Toronto was my sister and that she had written down the van's licence number. Love also made it clear that we were both expected home for dinner and if we didn't show, our parents would call the police. It seems they decided, instead of delaying their return, to take these two nutty teenagers back to Toronto earlier rather than later.

When we got to north Toronto, we said thank you for the ride, got out as fast as we could, and grabbed a Yonge streetcar down to Lawrence Park, where there was a phone booth and each of us called home. We were home for dinner, if a little late. We learned our lesson and warned all young teenagers not to climb into moving vans with strange men. You might end up in a pigpen.

Yonge Street Car—our main means of daily transportation.

Both Love and I tended to get detentions, mostly for disruptive behaviour. I confess I got more than Love did. One Saturday, Love had a three-hour detention and I had six hours. This meant, of course, that some poor staff member had to monitor me. After four boring hours, the teacher who monitored me informed me that I could go home and I, charming brat that I was, answered, "No, I still have two hours left of my detention." It seems that Miss Edith M. Read got news of Love's and my bad behaviour. Monday morning Love was called into the principal's office, and she returned a short time later with a smile on her face, declaring that she had just been put on probation by Miss Read. Then she asked, "Love, what is probation?"

I answered, "Not good, Love." Then it was my turn. We were each told that this was a warning and that we were to be separated. Love would be in 2A, because her marks were better than mine, and I would be moved to 2B. At that moment, I realized that it was very unfair of me to cause my poor mother so much worry.

Mother, who was bringing up three teenagers on a limited budget, had no social life with Father away in England because those were the days when a single woman in Mother's society was never included in a gathering of couples. Mother did have one very healthy outlet, however. She had several female friends, many of whom were single women, and all very much involved in the art world.

Several were members of the Toronto Heliconian Club, the only club in Toronto for women only that was not tied to an association such as the IODE (Imperial Order Daughters of the Empire). Housed at 35 Hazelton Avenue in Yorkville, this early church called Olivet was a perfect venue for this club of artists, writers, dancers, and other professionals or like-minded women of independent thought. Mother was a member and became president during the war. I think it saved her sanity.

Heliconian Hall—our Gothic-revival former church, now our women's art club named after the muses on Mount Helicon in Greece.

Mother decided to enrol Jimmy and Mary in a ballroom dance class given by a fellow Heliconian, Evelyn Van Valkenburg, since they were at the age where young people started to date and loved to dance. Of course, I didn't want to be left out, so I managed to get included. The class was a success and took place in the former Heliconian church hall with a grand piano accompaniment. Unfortunately, Evelyn Van Valkenburg, Mary, and Jimmy were not pleased with my behaviour. Evidently, I constantly disrupted the class with my clowning and was firmly invited to leave.

Love and I both realized that it was about time that we started to grow up. We behaved impeccably well (in our opinion) for the rest of Grade 9.

When the school year was over, Love went off to a camp for Jewish girls, and Mother somehow managed to scrape together enough money to send Mary and me to Camp Tanamakoon for a month. Tanamakoon was in Algonquin Park. Miss Hamilton was the director and ran a disciplined camp. She attempted to pick her counsellors very carefully and almost was successful. I will quote verbatim from letters I sent Mother from camp.

"Yesterday I got back to camp after the most super three-day canoe and ranging trip I could ever hope to have. There were six of us including a counsellor, a C.I.T. (counsellor in training) and four campers. We laughed continually, sang songs, and talked in Scottish and Irish dialects (all six of us). We built a john (W.C. to you). It was rather primitive. First, we picked a secluded spot in the woods, dug a hole and built a narrow bench above. Our counsellor Joan Christie, a B.S.S. (Bishop Straughn School) senior is a handsome tall girl, She and I are the most enthusiastic. She is the most skilled but I like to show off, especially to her who I find very attractive, and after paddling to a deserted lumber camp on Head Lake I almost single-handedly ripped five planks off the bunks in the hut and we hauled them over a mile portage and to our canoes and then managed to balance them on the gunwalls of the canoes and paddle them to the Boundary Lake camp site's dock. Then we sawed them to the correct length to fit our dock. They were devilish and hard to saw and later to hammer. The lumbermen used very hard wood. We used a brace and a bit to hammer the planks into our dock.

Mom, I believe I've finally found a handcraft that I like and I'm good at. I can be your handyman. Also, I learned how to gunnelbob. This is done by standing barefoot on the rear gunnels and propelling the canoe forward by squatting down while moving arms and buttocks also forward and backward in rhythmic movements."

***

Later in life, when most of my former high school friends were taking to the ski hills, I was, whenever possible, moving on the stage. I regret having not become a skier since I've always been the right build, have strong thigh muscles, and had pretty good balance on canoe gunnels. I would have enjoyed the thrill of skiing down a mountain, as Love did. But the stage fascinated me more.

There was to be a play. I wanted to be a part of it and was content with the small part of St. Francis of Assisi. I admired the actress who played Joan of Arc. She was a few years older than I, a B.S.S. girl with blond shoulder-length hair, Charmion King. I found her quite beautiful and liked the way she moved and thought she was convincing. I realized then that when I grew up, I wanted to be an actress.

Sheila in character as St. Francis Assisi, skit at camp.

That August at Camp Tanamakoon was memorable for another reason. Father was returning home after over two years overseas. Mary and I were so excited when Mother and Father arrived at the dock. Dad told me later that I practically knocked him down when I leaped on him when he first arrived. Although I hated that camp was almost at an end, I looked forward to returning to Toronto now that Daddy had finally come home.

Father in uniform at basic training camp in Newmarket. The portrait is by my mother, Grace Craig.

Unfortunately, all was not well. Mother had been very quiet about her health, but it was obvious, if I had bothered to look, that she was not a bit well. What she had not told us was that she had been diagnosed with a tumour of the kidney. I must confess that, as a teenager, I had no concept of what that meant. The adolescent brain, in my case at least, was lacking. Father, it turned out, was home on compassionate leave because he had been told Mother was to have surgery to remove her kidney. This was 1944 and, although back then it was thought medicine was very advanced, compared to now, it was in its adolescence. Mother had her operation, and the surgeon removed not only her kidney but her gallbladder as well, which was full of stones. Back then there were no stomach pumps, and when Mother was post-op, her very intelligent nurse noticed that she was groaning in pain. The nurse who normally followed protocol and was unable to reach the surgeon decided on her own, as she thought she would lose her patient otherwise. She caused Mother to vomit, and the result relieved her patient, who otherwise probably would have died. Mother recovered quite quickly and lived another forty-four years in remarkably good health.

Mother and Father on the terrace at Dawlish. They were happy because Mother was almost fully recovered from her life-threatening surgery.

By this time, I was in Grade 11. I took lessons in voice production from the Royal Conservatory's vocal teacher Clara Salisbury Baker. I especially enjoyed readings of Shakespeare, although it was difficult, and certainly preferred voice lessons to piano lessons. Love was active with the library and music, and I was interested in theatre.

I had become friends with another classmate, Anne Whyte. Anne lived in a very large house at 202 Roxborough Drive which backs on the ravine at the intersection of Roxborough, Whitney and Binscarth.

The neighbourhood is quite posh, and Annie's father had managed very well during the Depression, which financially wiped out other men of his generation. He owned the Whyte Packing Company. He was a meat packer. Anne's eldest sibling was Jack, a captain in the Canadian Army, followed by Marg, then Bob, a private in the Canadian Army, and Robin. Anne's mother was brought up on a farm and was a splendid cook. She had disciplined four children and by the time Anne appeared, she said, "I've had enough and will let Anne do as she pleases," which is exactly what Anne has been doing ever since. That, no doubt, is what attracted my lifelong friend to me. She is an original. Just as Judy and I didn't fit the mold, nor did she. Anne asked me to visit her family cottage on the Island, situated between Ward's Island and Centre Island on the boardwalk. It was a large turn-of-the-century frame house painted green, rather impressive. We were adventurous, and in early October we dared one another to jump into Lake Ontario, which was just fifty metres away. It was very invigorating. Then Annie and I decided it was time to make a little pocket money. We heard Bell Telephone was looking for inward operators, so we applied for two weeks during the Christmas holidays. It paid very badly, but it was an interesting experience and I learned how to talk like my fellow inward operators. But my supervisor chastised me for answering long-distance calls, which I hadn't been trained to do. Nevertheless, on the Bell Christmas tree, when all the regular operators had received their exchange gifts, there was one left. Finally, my supervisor said, "Miss Craig, have you not looked at the tree?" I did, and there was a little gift to me from her. I felt a little sad that I had nothing for her.

January came with the worst snowstorm I have ever witnessed. It was so memorable, I wrote a poem to describe it. Here it is:

S'no Matter
Poem by Sheila Craig

T'was early morn of Tuesday last
When I awoke, a dreadful blast
Shook the windows, and banged the door,
And blew me almost to the floor.
On looking out the air was snow,
The sky above a pinkish glow.
The house across the street was gone.
The trees and hedges, and the lawn
Had disappeared with the storm
At seven o'clock last Tuesday morn.
Seven- o- five, the bus was due.
But would the T.T.C. come through?
Seven-thirty came and still no bus,
But get to school we simply muss. (poet's license)
We donned our skis without delay,
And straightway were on our way,
But found ourselves waist-deep in snow
But on to school we still must go.

Despite this age of gadgets new,
Nature prevails at times this true,
He must go back to Grandma's time
When snowshoeing was in its prime.

We were gay this wintry day.
As snowshoes sped us on our way.
Our exaltation reached its peak
When we reached the car lines rather weak
To find a street car waiting there,
The answer to a maiden's prayer.
When finally to school we came,
The atmosphere was not the same
as yesterday. The doors were locked.
No brass band? Why we were shocked?
A boarder yelled, "Why be a fool?
On such a day there is no school."

When the skis proved useless in the deep snow, Mary remembered that there were two pairs of snowshoes in the attic. So we retrieved them, and miraculously the leather bindings held.

Chapter 7

Finally, the war, which had lasted since September 1, 1939, was almost over with all its devastation and loss of lives, including many of Canada's young soldiers and Craig relatives. On a beautiful May morning, we were in class when, suddenly, from our little Calvin church next door, we heard the sound of bells, which were almost drowned out by the large bells on St. Paul's big Anglican church two blocks away on Bloor Street. Sirens started to sound, and car horns blared. Our entire class rose as Miss Read arrived at our door, and we all cheered as she announced the end of the war. The class was dismissed.

Love had arrived at school in her brand-new red convertible that her parents had given her for exemplary marks and prowess in music, or whatever the reason, and eight of us piled in. I sat with Whytey, as my good friend Annie was called, and Joan Heisey on the top of the rear seat in the open convertible. No one bothered us, including the police. When Mary and I came home, Father served us our first glass of sherry to celebrate. Until then, we were not allowed to drink anything alcoholic.

Neither Mary nor I wanted to continue as campers at Tanamakoon. We wanted some responsibility and didn't want our father to be burdened with the cost of camp. Annie told us that there was a new camp about to open in Haliburton that would be run by relatives of hers, and they were looking for C.I.T.s (counsellors in training) who were seventeen and had camp experience. The camp would be run by Major Hoyle and his family. His daughter Robin and his wife, Teddy, encouraged Annie to join because they wanted Annie's creative expertise and calculated that she would make a good counsellor, teaching children how to make things. I found Robin's husband interesting. He was keen on theatre and determined that one day his hometown, Stratford, with its river Avon, should become a Canadian version of England's Stratford-upon-Avon. His name was Tom Patterson. His determination was finally rewarded in 1953, and in 2023, a new Stratford theatre was completed and named the Tom Patterson Theatre.

Annie, Mary, and I were invited to join Camp Gay Venture as C.I.T.s. Mary wanted to be with her friends in a tent, and Annie and I wanted to share a tent, which we did and pitched it by the lake as far from the main lodge as we could. Although our interests were not the same, Annie created amazing bits of craft, more like jewellery, whereas I loved to canoe and wanted to explore.

Very soon I got the chance to explore the wilds of Haliburton. By the third week of camp, I had been on two short canoe trips, but the most memorable was the one that the memory of which makes me shudder today. I loved it. It was to last for five nights and six days. There were eight campers, two counsellors, and one C.I.T., me. On the third day, we split into two groups. Four campers remained with their counsellor and the guide to go fishing. Four adventurous campers, a counsellor, Janet Lewis (aka Lewie), and I set out to explore some of the vast regions of Haliburton. From there we attempted to find the opening into the "great Frieze" (pronounced freezy) river.

Annie (Whitey) pumping water with Sheila (Blackie) overseeing at Gay Venture camp. Both are C.I.Ts.

Annie with Robin Hoyle, camp leader and daughter of Major Hoyle and his wife Teddy.

Blackie and Whitey paddling canoe at Gay Venture Camp.

    At first, we came to a little river about the size of the Don. After much pushing and lifting, we finally had the canoes afloat in the river. For a while, we were able to paddle without much difficulty, but then we found the surrounding fallen trees that we had to portage over and began to wonder if maybe the Frieze river was not the quickest way to big Black Lake. After five miles of wading through muddy water (some shoulder high), we had to turn back as the river was completely overgrown.

    It turned out that much of the river water turned into liquid mud and there is a portage that takes its place. On the way home, we composed this song to the tune of "Oh! The Horse Went Around."

Squishy, Squeezy River Frieze

Oh! We paddled down the Frieze and we got stuck fast.

And Louie came first and Love came last.

And we pulled the canoes through mud up to our eyes

And we swatted mosquitos and we batted flies.

Oh, we pulled off bloodsuckers, pushed aside trees,

And we tore our panties and we scraped our knees

But we came out happy, and we gave three cheers.

If there's water in the Frieze, we'll go back some year.

Finally, we got back to our campsite on the shore, where we spent the night sleeping in the sand. This was a mistake. Sand is soft at first, but when you change position, it's hard as rocks. We attempted to paddle back to our first campsite on the fourth day and had to fight a stiff wind. Finally, worn out and happy, we just had time to get the kids' dinner when a heavy storm cloud approached. So, like the dopes we were, we unrolled our bed rolls, put ground sheets over top, and stuck our heads under a canoe. I started to madly bail my bed. That night we had a warm but damp sleep, spending a good part of it holding a ground sheet over our heads. I should add, back in the 1940s, tents weren't provided for campers on canoe trips. We had to sleep under the stars or in the rain. The only cover we had was the canoes.

The storm on the fifth day was pretty wild and we had hailstones as big as marbles. When we arrived back at the camp, we said we had had a marvellous time. Many years later, I look back and can't imagine anything more uncomfortable. It has been said that "Youth is wasted on the young." But in the case of these innocent but positive teenagers, I don't think so. Nothing wasted on them.

***

Perhaps I should have mentioned earlier that Branksome senior school was divided into clans. Mary was in the MacGregor clan, and I chose Douglas. In Grade 12, my fellow clan members had voted me in as their sub-chieftain. Obviously, this would not have been allowed if the staff had any say, but they didn't. It's odd how being given a position of responsibility, even as minimal as this, caused a change in my attitude.

It was 1947, my last year of high school, Grade 13. I had begun to take life more seriously as the Douglas clan chieftain, which entailed some responsibility. Mother had recovered from her serious surgery, and I started to realize that life was more than a series of childish adventures. Love was involved in her work in the school library and piano lessons, and I became more involved in drama with my vocal teacher, Clara Salisbury Baker.

Once a year, the school put on a serious play. That year, they chose J. M. Barrie's *The Admirable Crichton*, an odd choice for an all-girls school since, of the seventeen characters, only seven were female roles. Some of the girls were tall; I was barely five foot four and was pleasantly surprised when asked to play the title role of the Admirable Crichton. My leading lady was at least two or three inches taller than I. Although being caught smoking on campus was a serious offence, curiously, it was allowed on stage, which is certainly not the case now. My father showed me how to light a pipe and I was upset when the audience laughed when I lit my pipe on the stage. However, I managed to be convincing as an English butler and the play was a success.

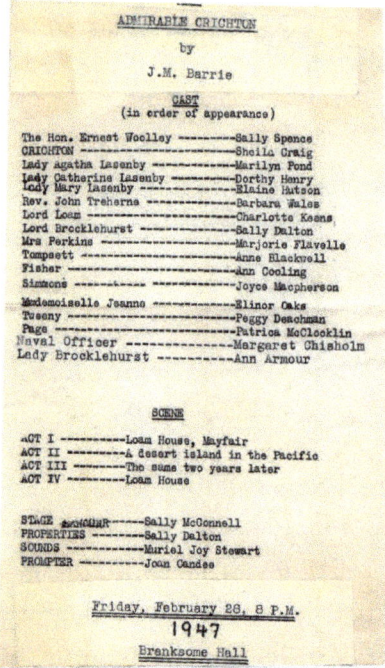

```
                ADMIRABLE CRICHTON
                        by
                    J.M. Barrie
                       CAST
                (in order of appearance)

The Hon. Ernest Woolley --------Sally Spence
CRICHTON -----------------------Sheila Craig
Lady Agatha Lasenby ------------Marilyn Pond
Lady Catherine Lasenby ---------Dorthy Henry
Lady Mary Lasenby --------------Elaine Hutson
Rev. John Treherne -------------Barbara Wales
Lord Loam ----------------------Charlotte Keens
Lord Brocklehurst --------------Sally Dalton
Mrs Perkins --------------------Marjorie Flavelle
Tompsett -----------------------Anne Blackwell
Fisher -------------------------Ann Cooling
Simmons ------------------------Joyce Macpherson
Mademoiselle Jeanne ------------Elinor Oaks
Tweeny -------------------------Peggy Deachman
Page ---------------------------Patricia McClocklin
Naval Officer ------------------Margaret Chisholm
Lady Brocklehurst --------------Ann Armour

                      SCENE
ACT I   ----------Loam House, Mayfair
ACT II  ----------A desert island in the Pacific
ACT III ----------The same two years later
ACT IV  ----------Loam House

STAGE MANAGER------Sally McConnell
PROPERTIES --------Sally Dalton
SOUNDS ------------Muriel Joy Stewart
PROMPTER ----------Joan Candee

              Friday, February 28, 8 P.M.
                      1947
                  Branksome Hall
```

The Admirable Crichton program, showing Sheila Craig in the title role.

When summer arrived, Annie was not invited back to Camp Gay Venture as a counsellor. Evidently, she was a bit too casual and, on two occasions, left her seven- and eight-year-old boys to fend for themselves for half an hour, a definite no-no. There were no accidents or incidents. I thought the Hoyles' were too rigid, but I learned that the camp was liable if anything happened. I was given the awesome responsibility of the tripping counsellor. Major Hoyle asked if I would give him a lesson in paddling. He was an excellent student, but frankly, I was a little nervous when asked to paddle two nervous parents, neither of whom could swim, across the lake on a breezy day to their visitors' accommodation. I was relieved that the lodge they were staying in brought them back in a motor launch.

Part 2

University, 1947–1950

Chapter 8

I was sad to leave my youthful camping days behind me, but excited about going to university. Judy's parents sent her to McGill in Montreal. Of my classmates entering U of T (University of Toronto), they were almost equally divided between choosing St. Hilda's College, which was affiliated with the Anglican Church, or Victoria College, which was affiliated with the United Church. I chose UC (University College). My reason for this choice was that I had heard it had the best drama section. I made a good choice.

I felt I was a new person. The campus was exciting. The University College building was like nothing that I had ever seen before, with its unique facade and gargoyle niches. The majority of my female classmates were Jewish, and they were a lively lot.

Probably my last act of disreputable childish behaviour was in late September, when one of my classmates invited me to join five other girls to pose for a photo smoking cigars on the formal front steps of University College. Unfortunately, the incident was picked up by one of the newspapers, and within twenty-four hours, I had a phone call from Ainsley McMichael more or less ordering me to appear at 19 Elm Avenue in the Branksome Hall principal's office. I dutifully attended, was thoroughly chastised, and agreed to behave "the way a Branksome graduate should."

Perhaps you are wondering why I never had a boyfriend in high school and why I constantly had crushes mainly on older girls. I don't think it was because I was basically a lesbian, although I certainly had the tendencies. I believe it was because, for the most part, the boys I met during my early youth were uninteresting and predictable and, frankly, so WASP. Now here I was in university, and suddenly, I discovered men. It wasn't just that the high school boys were now at university; it was something else.

The war had ended in the late summer of 1945, and after demobilization, the young soldiers, sailors, and airmen were given the opportunity of having a free university education offered only to veterans. Many took advantage of this offer. My professors were all men. They were polite and addressed me as Miss Craig. Most of the high school graduates went to Trinity College, Victoria College, or Saint Michael's College, but University College appeared to be the choice for many of the returning armed forces. I was in my element.

Most of my former schoolmates from Branksome who went to Victoria College and St. Hilda's College, the female counterpart of Trinity College, adopted the 1947 dress style of bobby socks and saddle shoes, and carried their textbooks in front of them, whereas I wore shoes with a small heel and buckle strap, and I carried my books in a briefcase and wore my hair in a chignon. I felt quite at home in my new environment. I loved university.

Social and Philosophical Studies as a four-year course appealed to me. But the subjects I chose for my first year weren't all favourites. English was a delight, especially since I found my teacher, a young assistant professor, very handsome — a blond Adonis. He was Vincent Tovell, nephew of Vincent Massey, who, at the time, was Chancellor of U of T. Since a foreign language was mandatory, I chose French. The lectures were at 9:00 a.m., which was a blow. My other subjects were Psychology, Philosophy, Art, and Archaeology. Psychology was very easy. Granted it was only the first year, but I couldn't understand why simple truths I felt I'd always known were given such fancy names and titles. Philosophy, on the other hand, I found difficult. It was logic, taught by the highly esteemed Professor Marcus Long, and I didn't get it, but I found Art and Archeology fascinating.

I especially loved Charles Comfort as a teacher. He had been in action as a Canadian war artist from 1939 to 1945. Amongst other things, he taught Venetian art using egg tempera as a medium, as Duccio in early painting had. Sad to say I failed to keep any of my artwork.

During this time, I made some friends; one of them was a fellow student in my psychology class. His name was John Howe, and we hit it off instantly. He was one of the Armed Forces members who took advantage of the free university education offered to returning veterans. He came from a very humble background. His father was a caretaker, and his mom was a cleaning lady. No one in his family went beyond high school. They would have preferred that he get a job instead of going to university. But John was determined. He entered UC at twenty-one as the youngest captain in the Canadian Army.

I was a little envious of John and his uniform, as I was always fond of uniforms. When I read a notice posted on campus that the Red Cross was anxiously seeking volunteers to escort wounded Armed Forces veterans to therapy at Sunnybrook and back, and that the drivers would wear a Red Cross uniform and be able to drive a vehicle with a double gearshift, I couldn't resist. After a short time of driving disabled veterans, I found the job very rewarding, especially when some of them requested me as their driver. Driving occupied two afternoons a week, which was all right.

John and I had several interests in common. We had a passion for theatre. When I switched from Philosophy to Anthropology, John was already in the course. We would meet in the common room and walk together up Philosopher's Walk to the Royal Ontario Museum (ROM), where our Anthropology lectures took place in the theatre auditorium. Our professor, Edmond Carpenter, better known as Professor Ted, was inspired by Margaret Mead, her fieldwork in Samoa, and her original views and fascination with the Trobriand Islanders. Mead was said to have intellectual restlessness, a trait also shared by our favourite young Professor Ted. He was so interesting that students from other courses and colleges sometimes came to his lectures.

I heard there was an audition for a one-act play. I met the director, a tall slender, dark-haired young man with a beautiful rather than handsome face. He asked me about my acting experience. I blushed since it was so limited, but then told him the year before I played the lead in another J. M. Barrie play, *The Admirable Crichton*, at Branksome Hall. He smiled, suppressing a laugh, then said the part he was casting was of a French maid, a coquette, very feminine. I gulped since I had no idea how to be a coquette. I read the lines. There weren't very many. He looked at me and said, "You look fine for the part, but you'll have to retrain your brain. Forget you ever went to an all-girls school and think of yourself as a simple French girl attempting to rise in the servants' world by charming the male employers. And remember the play is a comedy." Somehow, I got the part and, for the first time in my eighteen years on this earth, when I put on my costume, I was terrified. But when I went on stage, I became a French maid who was also a coquette, and the audience laughed.

My director, Murray Davis, must have liked me because the next play he directed, he cast me in a leading role as the mother in J. M. Barrie's play *A Well-Remembered Voice*. By this time, I had a serious crush on the young man, even though I was told he was queer. The term "gay" for homosexuals was not used in 1947. As I was about to enter the stage, Murray kissed me on the cheek for good luck, and I temporarily froze but recovered and all was well.

Also in my first year, I became friends with another first-year student, a graduate of Bishop Strachan School, Susi Davidson, who chose UC for much the same reason as I did. Her interest was in writing comedy skits for revue shows. I auditioned for both the UC Follies and the big revue show, the Varsity Follies. I was accepted and I enjoyed the small parts I was given and the dance routines.

I continued to have vocal lessons with my drama teacher, which gave me confidence. In the fall, I was invited back to Branksome to help with the senior year's performance of *The Importance of Being Earnest*. I got a credit in the program as the makeup artist. I decided to try radio and auditioned with a senior U of T student, Arthur Hiller, who produced and directed most of the campus radio plays. Arthur and I got along very well, and I thoroughly enjoyed campus radio shows. I still remember my first role, playing a small boy. Arthur Hiller later made a big career in the USA as a Hollywood film director.

In October, I auditioned for the director of Hart House Theatre, Bob Gill, for a role in the annual varsity production. It was *The Skin of Our Teeth* by Thornton Wilder. I was delighted to be offered the role of the Fortune Teller. The production ran for a week to full houses, and we all had excellent reviews. I continued with varsity radio for the balance of my time in university. Since the audience couldn't see me, my talent as a character actress allowed me to play everything from animals to headmistresses and even witches. John directed the UC entry *Overlaid*, which won the Inter-Varsity Play Award.

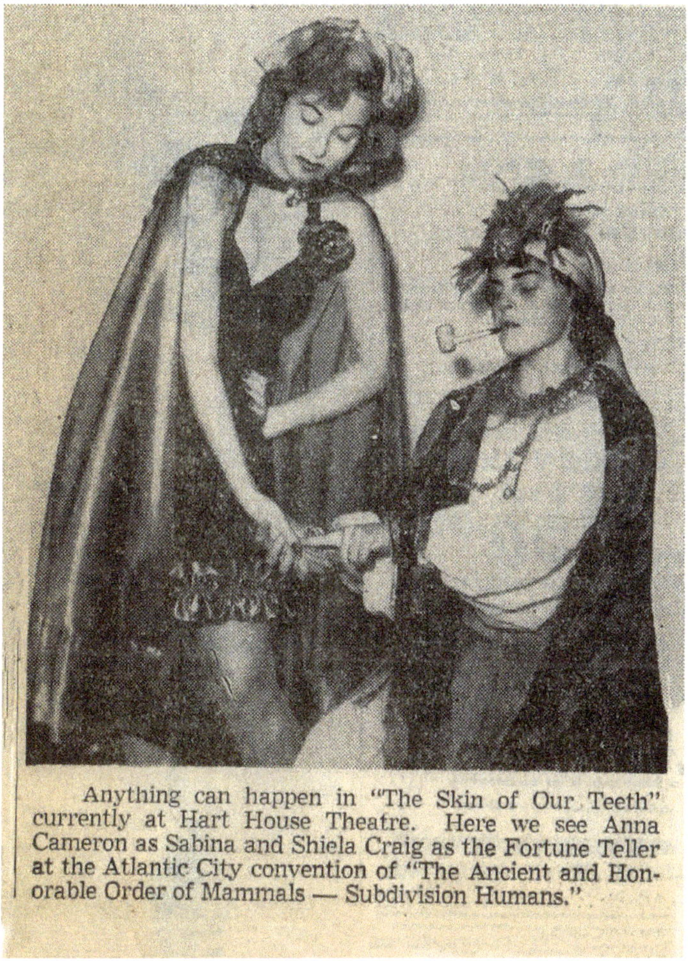

Anything can happen in "The Skin of Our Teeth" currently at Hart House Theatre. Here we see Anna Cameron as Sabina and Shiela Craig as the Fortune Teller at the Atlantic City convention of "The Ancient and Honorable Order of Mammals — Subdivision Humans."

The Skin of Our Teeth performed at Hart House Theatre, University of Toronto. (See caption in the image.)

Mr. and Mrs. President

—Varsity Staff Photo By Don Forgie

Mr. and Mrs. Antrobus (Eric House and Audrie Lowrie) officiating at the Convention of the Ancient and Honourable Order of Mammals, Subdivision Humans, in Atlantic City. A scene from Thornton Wilder's, THE SKIN OF OUR TEETH, the first Hart House Theatre production of this season which opened on Saturday.

Mr. and Mrs. President from *The Skin of Our Teeth*. (See caption in the image.)

I didn't have much time left over for studying, and my marks, especially in French, reflected that. Unfortunately, Drama as a subject, let alone a university course, didn't exist until much later. However, I thoroughly enjoyed my Fine Arts course and found Archeology fascinating. My favourite subject, probably due to the professor, was Anthropology.

Also in my second year, John and I were given an assignment by our Psychology professor: to go to the settlement house next to the Grange in downtown Toronto, where mostly immigrant children of the neighbourhood would congregate. Many of these children had suffered during or immediately after the war and were traumatized. Our assignment was to help them get over their trauma by having them act out their suffering and help them recover. This was so successful that we were disappointed when the assignment was finished.

At the end of my second year, I heard that a professional theatre company was looking for a few acting hopefuls to join as apprentices for the summer stock season in Peterborough. I applied and was accepted but was told there were no minor roles for women in the season's lineup. But it was a foot in the door. Peterborough Summer Theatre was founded by two young men, a Canadian with experience on the English and American stages, Michael Sadlier, who joined forces with a Montrealer who left radio script writing in New York to open the first of six major summer theatres to operate in Canada. The theatre was established in the modern Queen Mary School auditorium, which has a glass-walled foyer and a handsome theatre. The opening play, *Fortune My Foe*, was written by leading Canadian playwright Robertson Davies, who was also the editor of the *Peterborough Examiner*. He was the director of the play that had been chosen as the best play in the Dominion Drama Festival the year before. As an apprentice, I would get a lot of theatre experience, not necessarily as an actress.

When I arrived, I was told to go through town with a form of sandwich board to advertise the first production. Then I was to go backstage and see what was needed. It seems there was no costume mistress, and no one volunteered. I figured I was probably the least qualified, but I was told I was it. Then I, who hated "female handicraft," as I called it, was also given the job of seamstress and was told to alter Joy Lafleur's costume for *Blithe Spirit*. Then I was told to take my turn at the box office selling tickets. When the opening night was approaching, I was asked to do makeup, which I was totally unqualified to do, but I used my knowledge from Charles Comfort's art classes, where we learned to mix colours, and the result was rather good.

We had a few interesting old, seasoned actors, as well as Olive de Wilton, the wife of Boris Karloff, who was the original monster in *Frankenstein*. Olive was superstitious. She scolded me for whistling backstage since it was bad luck. There was another old actor, Bramwell Fletcher, from the 1930s movies, and I enjoyed hearing their theatre stories. In addition, there was a very young actor named Anthony Perkins who was just starting. He is best remembered for his clean-cut all-American boy next door image, and for his performance as the insane murderer who poses his dead mother in a sitting position in front of a second-floor window for all to see and then stabs Janet Leigh through a shower curtain in Alfred Hitchcock's horror movie *Psycho*. Janet Leigh was so traumatized that, afterward, she would never go in a shower.

I was considered very reliable for a while. But then Anna Cameron loaned me her father's car to do an errand. Anna was very particular about who was allowed to drive the car, and I was flattered. As I was about to step back into it after the errand, a fellow apprentice, the black sheep of the well-known Taschereau family, jumped in, turned on the ignition, and drove maybe forty feet before running into a public utility truck. I was devastated. Just as a policeman was arriving, Taschereau confessed he had no driver's licence. When the policeman asked who was driving, I, like a young fool, said I was. Anna and Michael Sadlier were very angry with me. They believed that I was the driver.

My father was very angry with me until I finally confessed my lie to him. And he was angrier with me for what fool I was. But he was especially furious with Taschereau when I told him the truth about what had occurred. My father was a man of honour and he found Taschereau's behaviour reprehensible. When I told John what had happened, he shook his head, but when I added that Taschereau was gay and I was told that he had described me as the original Sappho from the island of Lesbos, which I believe he considered a compliment, John laughed. I didn't particularly care and considered it just one more aspect of summer stock theatre. As for the accident with the car, there was no damage to Anna's father's car. It turned out that the chief executive officer of the public utility truck was a friend of my father's and they decided to go after Taschereau for the cost of the repair to the utility truck, which was $65. Taschereau said he couldn't afford the cost, but with the help of his priest, he managed to pay the money to my father who, after discussing it with his public utilities friend, returned the money to Taschereau, hoping that he had learned his lesson.

Then there was the humiliating episode when the cast thought it would be fun to get me drunk. I was not used to drinking hard liquor. They poured me two strong drinks of rum and Coke, which I had never had before, and I became very drunk. Someone drove me home to my pretty clapboard house. The sweet straitlaced landlady was asleep. I just made it to my room, but not to the bathroom, and spilt the contents of my stomach on my pristine white blanket. I felt terrible, passed out, and only woke up when the phone rang. The irate voice of director Robertson Davies admonished me and ordered me to get to the theatre immediately. It was a dress rehearsal, and as his assistant, it was my job to prompt the actors.

My third misdemeanour was when I swept the stage for opening night. I mistook a can of golden ochre paint for the cleaning product dust bane. Fortunately, the play was a comedy rather than a tragedy. I was sure I was going to get the sack, but Michael Sadlier let it pass. I did manage to get a small part in *By Candlelight in August*, so I did get to act. After that not-so-illustrious summer stock beginning of my professional stage career, it was time to go back to university.

However, my good friend Annie was about to be married. When Annie asked me to be her maid of honour, I had no idea what that entailed. John had recently bought an ancient, but not antique, car. I swear its maximum speed was not more than fifty miles per hour. The day of the wedding was the day after the final performance, so first thing in the morning, John drove me from Peterborough to Toronto in "Little Jo," as the car was called, and I had barely time to change my clothes before the wedding. I was no help to Annie to be ready for the big moment.

Chapter 9

In January 1949, John Howe directed an all-varsity studio presentation of *Murder in the Cathedral*. It was so successful that the critic suggested, due to its high calibre, it should be done as a full-scale production. I was proud of my friend's prowess.

In February 1949, the Inter-Varsity Drama Festival, with the universities of McMaster, Western, and Toronto, participated in presenting four plays in Hart House Theatre. U of T's entry was *Overlaid* by Robertson Davies, directed by John Howe. The one-act play took place in a farm kitchen. The play was static, but the two major players were John Walker (later Professor Walker) as an old farmer who longs for culture, and his shrewish puritanical middle-aged daughter, played by Edith Greenberg. Both were excellent. I had a short but funny part of the radio voice of Mrs. August Belmont. We also put on Bernard Shaw's play *Press Cuttings* about suffragettes. E. G. Wanger, the drama critic, gave an excellent revue and he said of me that I seemed to have stepped out of an 1890s fashion magazine, and I was a masterpiece of restrained burlesquing.

For the second successive year, a Robertson Davies play was presented. I designed and built the simple sets as well as directed the *Voice of the People*. Bob Osborne played Sharty and John Howe was the electrician, Sam.

The stage set of *Voice of the People* with Bob Osborne and John Howe. Set design by Sheila Craig, who also directed.

It was the autumn of 1949, my third year. Except for French, my marks were high seconds and one or two firsts. Art and Archeology was my honours four-year course, as was Anthropology. I read for Hart House Theatre's director Robert Gill. The play was one of my favourites, *Romeo and Juliet*. Why, in Shakespeare's day, were women not allowed to perform? Of the four female parts, my preference was for the nurse. Sadly, the part was cast the day before, as was Lady Capulet. The leading role of Juliet was wrong for me, and it was to be played by Charmion King, whom I had admired at Camp Tanamakoon. Only Lady Montague was left, with one line and a scream. So I was Lady Montague. I made the most of the scream, but I was sad not to play the nurse, although I had to admit the actress who played her was excellent. I did enjoy the UC Follies and the Varsity Review but especially Varsity Radio with Art Hiller.

Then John got his choice for UC's entry in the varsity one-act play competition. The play was to be Jean-Paul Sartre's *No Exit*. It was decided that John Howe would be the director and the valet and would lead the three major characters into a claustrophobic room where they would spend the rest of eternity together. I would play the Lesbian, Christopher Taylor would play the Coward, and Patricia Scott would be the Nymphomaniac. We took the play very seriously and considered it a morality play.

However, Dr. William Robert Taylor, Principal of UC, a somewhat sanctimonious gentleman, banned the production on the University College Players Guild's Stage without any explanation, deciding it was not suitable for university students. I remember thinking that if it wasn't suitable for university students, then what would it be suitable for? Remember that homosexuality was only legalized in 1969. It was decided that we should use the Hart House Theatre's stage instead. Then, just as we were figuring out how to adapt the scene to the larger Hart House stage, John was informed that the University Drama Guild, after a discussion with Robert Gill and others, decided not to allow us to perform the play in Hart House Theatre. We were dismayed, especially by Bob Gill's acquiescence, but realized that he was between a rock and a hard place.

In the meantime, several Toronto newspapers got involved, as well as some people whose names are familiar even now, and John made a note of the names of people who added their comments, condemning the narrow-minded outlook of those in charge. I'm going to attach the list of names that John recorded. Many of you who are older will recognize them.

E. G. Wanger, Langdon Dixon, John Walker, Herbert Whittaker, Jack Ferguson, Eric Holdenby, Rose MacDonald, Prof. Fackenheim, Harold Burk, Jack Carr, Prof. Northrop Fry, Murray Paulin, Bill Sleneak, John Coulter, Prof. Ted Carpenter, Jim Taylor, B. K. Sandwell, William Crichton, Miss Ferguson, Lister Sinclair, Harry Long, Prof. McAndrew, Mel Breen, Bruce Evoy, Prof. Bagnani, Dora Mavor Moore

"No Exit"

BANNED AT U.C ALSO

THE VARSITY

No Reason Given, Ban To Remain

Editorial:

No Exit..

Thus spake Principal Taylor:
"One of the leaders in the councils of the United Nations said recently, '. . . . There is no doubt in my mind but that moral authority—moral force—is the only force that can accomplish great things in the world.' Need I say that society can rightly expect in these times that a major portion of this indispensable moral authority will be supplied by university trained men and women."

Thus spake Principal Taylor in his message to the Class of '49, printed in the latest annual University College Bulletin.

This emphasis of the Principal's on university trained men and women as dispensers of moral authority is especially interesting at this time. The Principal has given no reason for his cancellation of "No Exit." In view of recent events the most valid assumption open to us is that the cancellation is on "moral grounds."

If the assumption is correct, then obviously Principal Taylor cannot rightly expect what he claims society can rightly expect. If one believes that University students are possessors of high ideals and considerable moral force, one would not expect students to waste time producing an immoral play. Further, such a person would not expect other students to go to see an immoral play.

To cancel the play on moral grounds is to express a disbelief in the moral strength of students. For Principal Taylor to express this disbelief is for him to exhibit a lack of moral conviction, and so to stand as a poor example of moral authority to undergraduates.

We hope the Principal cancelled the play for reasons other than moral ones, and we wish he would state what his reasons are.

.... No Entrance

Initially to have been performed at the University College Players' Guild Stage (not allowed) then at Hart House Theatre (once again banned).

When Mother, who had read *No Exit*, which most of the others had not, heard this, she immediately called the president of the Toronto Heliconian Club, and within hours arranged that we could stage *No Exit* on its tiny stage. Because the play is set in one claustrophobic room, this was ideal. Because of fire regulations, the hall could only accommodate just over one hundred people. Early in March, our entry was performed in Heliconian Hall, with some twenty people standing at the rear of the house and a substantial number outside, unable to enter. The reasons for this crowd were, in some cases, academic or political, including those who felt the injustice of a university being unable to accept unusual philosophies. Some also came because of the sensational publicity, hoping to see a dirty play. They must have been disappointed. We charged seventy-five cents for a ticket that covered the rental of the hall, plus we divided the balance four ways. I took home eleven dollars.

Now in our third year, John and I felt very much at home in our surroundings, especially in the ROM's theatre. After our Anthropology lecture, which took place in the late afternoon, Professor Carpenter would often be joined by professors who liked to spend an hour or so discussing the world situation or some other important issues over a beer or two. The problem was that the local "watering hole" in the basement of the Park Plaza Hotel, known as the King Cole Room men's section, was very noisy and disruptive. For the professors to drink beer in civilized surroundings, they would have to be accompanied by a woman. For all the feminists who might be reading this, the mixed-sex King Cole Room was one of the very few advantages offered to a female back then. The professors would buy me one beer, which was all I could drink, bearing in mind that I was underage for drinking.

After an hour or so of fascinating conversation, John and I would take the Bloor streetcar and transfer to the Yonge streetcar, where he would get off at the Summerhill station and I would continue to the Eglinton station and take the bus home to brush my teeth so Father wouldn't smell the beer when he came home. Mother wanted to hear all about what I had learned and admitted that she was slightly jealous. If it hadn't been for the beer drinking with me underage, I'm sure Dad would have been delighted that his daughter was getting additional knowledge.

Susi Davidson, my UC pal who wrote skits, etc. for the UC players and the All-Varsity Revue.

Varsity Follies was now called the All-Varsity Review. One skit I was cast in, and which Susi wrote, was the part of a French swordfish. This fish had green makeup on the arms and legs, and I wore a stunning beaded, red silk dress from Paris that my mother had worn on her honeymoon at the Fairmont Le Château Frontenac in Quebec City. The part required a European French accent. I was in my element since the one thing Madame Perry taught me at Branksome was how to speak with a proper French accent. I liked that dress with all its beads. Many years later, when my mother was in her late nineties, she gave the dress to a young woman who admired it when she visited my mother. Sometime later I spotted a familiar-looking dress in a vintage shop window. I asked to see it, examined the hem and there was the telltale green makeup. The price tag was $1,000. The next time I passed the shop the dress was gone.

***

In early spring 1950, I had a call from someone at the Arts & Letters Club. My father had been a member of this prestigious all-male club since 1934. The only time females were allowed to enter its walls, other than the kitchen and cleaning staff, was when the club put on its plays and graciously allowed women to play the female roles. I was invited to be part of a play written by club member John Coulter. Born in 1888 in Belfast, he was a playwright and broadcaster who had immigrated to Canada and moved to Toronto, where he married Olive Clare Primrose, a short story writer and poet. They had two daughters, including Clare Coulter, who is now a highly thought-of actress. *The Drums Are Out* was one of his twenty-two plays that the club chose to enter in the Provincial Drama Festival.

The Drums Are Out is the story of a young schoolteacher, Jean, who is torn between two loyalties, to her father, a sergeant in the Belfast police force, and to her husband, a leader of the rebels. I was to play the role of the young schoolteacher heroine. I felt so in sympathy with Jean that I almost forgot I was acting.

In the receiving line after the final evening Saturday and the presentations are Roy Stewart, president of the Central Ontario Drama League; Maxwell Wray, adjudicator; Mrs. Stewart and festival director Dr. Kenneth Levinson.

The Dignitaries (See caption.)

John Coulter.
Winner of the medal for the best Canadian author of play at festival. Play, The Drums Are Out, has its action in West Belfast room during period of "the troubles."

Irish-born John Coulter, prominent dramatist, member of the Arts & Letters Club, and a truly remarkable human being. (See caption.)

The cast of *The Drums Are Out.*

Winner of the trophy for the best directed play, The Drums Are Out, was W. S. Milne seen with Sheila Craig who played the leading woman's role in the Arts and Letters Club production.

W. S. Milne and the author. (See caption.)

> Friday, March 10th, and Saturday, March 11th, 1950
> **THE ARTS AND LETTERS CLUB**
> PRESENTS
>
> # "The Drums Are Out"
>
> by JOHN COULTER
>
> ★ ★ ★
>
> CAST — In Order of Appearance
>
> | | |
> |---|---|
> | Mrs. Sheridan | Irene Henderson |
> | Sergeant Thomas Sheridan, her husband, of the Royal Ulster Constabulary | George Savin |
> | Jean, their daughter | Sheila Craig |
> | Constable Nixon, R.U.C. | Robert D. Allworth |
> | Matt McCann, a pigeon-fancier, neighbour of the Sheridans | Hugh Watson |
> | Denis Patterson, an I.R.A. gunman | John Watson |
> | A Black-and-Tan | Stanley Cooper |
> | An R.U.C. Constable | H. L. Deacon |

The program for *The Drums Are Out*.

I enjoyed rehearsing in Hart House Theatre and looked forward to the performance. My directors were John Coulter and W. S. Milne. All went well until I made the mistake of bringing home my costume, which had been designed and made by the wife of W. S. Milne, the prime director.

Mother took one look and recoiled in horror. The dress was ankle-length in red cotton with a large white collar. It looked rather attractive to me. Mother announced that it was entirely wrong for the era of the play's action and clashed with the set, which was in beige and brown tones. Mother insisted that I wear a calf-length brown skirt and a yellow flannel shirt. It was the right colour and era but didn't do much for me. I was worried and asked John Coulter what I should do. He didn't seem to want to be involved. Opening night arrived. I was about to set out for the theatre in plenty of time for makeup and costume discussion and last-minute instructions. Mother handed me the director's wife's red costume, which she had carefully taken apart.

So, in fear and trepidation, I arrived at the theatre and received a blast from W. S. Milne, whose hostile presence I expected. His large wife looked devastated, and I was embarrassed. I put on my mother's choice and tried to clear my mind. Fortunately, I was so in sympathy with my character that I soon forgot the costume fiasco and immersed myself in the role. It wasn't easy because I couldn't help overhearing W. S. Milne speaking to Maxwell Wray, the educator, saying, "Do not give the best actress award to Sheila Craig." The educator gave the best actress award to Sylvie Page for her role in *Awake and Sing!* but he gave me a very nice review.

Shortly thereafter, I had a phone call from the head of the University College French department, Professor François Jeanneret, later chancellor of the university. I was surprised. He said, "Miss Craig, I'm phoning you because I'm concerned that you are about to fail your final French exam. I realize that you have devoted most of your university life to the stage and, because of late hours, have missed many French lectures along with your colleague, Miss Davidson. I wish to help you and Miss Davidson. My reason is twofold. You are not aware of the fact, but my best friend and colleague throughout the 1914 to 1918 war in Belgium and France was your uncle Ramsay Morris, and your family and mine are neighbours. I also appreciate what you and Miss Davidson contributed to university life. I am willing to offer the two of you three evening French lessons at Glengowan, my house. This does not mean that you will pass, but it should encourage you to study."

So, Susi and I dutifully attended and even did some studying. We each managed just to pass with 61 or 62 percent. Incidentally, the exam did not contain any information that Professor Jeanneret had given us in the three intensive evening lessons.

When it came to English, my best subject, I had forgotten all about timing and wrote a very interesting essay, totally ignoring the deadline, and when the bell rang and the time was up, I had only written less than 60 percent of the paper. Needless to say, I failed. I would have to write a sup.

***

I had recently auditioned for a summer job with the producer Brian Doherty, a Toronto lawyer, and was accepted to join a musical review in a barn adapted to a theatre. It was called the Red Barn Theatre at Jackson's Point on Lake Simcoe. I joined the troupe. The first show, *Crazy with the Heat,* which opened in very cool weather on Dominion Day, featured original music, lyrics, and all Canadian material.

Of the thirty-five members of the troupe, there were many young performers. According to Herbert Whittaker, a drama critic who reviewed the opening night, the show was strongest musically and very catchy. As well as singing, we also danced. All the routines were directed by an experienced professional, Gladys Forrester, who was also the lead dancer. I was able to do the Charleston, so well, in fact, that I could do double time for about twenty seconds.

We rehearsed all day and early evening and performed the show at night. After rehearsing all day, it was great to go for a swim in Lake Simcoe, which was just fifty metres from the rather humble old-frame hotel that housed the cast. The day after the opening of each of the four shows was the only time off during the entire eight weeks. I had no time to study for my sup. I thanked God daily that the sup was not French.

There was a lot of musical talent at the Red Barn, especially in the creative field. Roy Wolvin was the chief songwriter, and Dusty Davis, a seasoned pro, did most of the arrangements and played the piano for the Barnstormers, which was what we were called. I still remember the tunes and even the lyrics for most of them; they were *Crazy with the Heat, Winnipeg, Looking for a Man*, and *No Place Twice*. There were altogether four shows, each lasting two weeks.

CANADIAN THEMES provide material for revues. In this Winnipeg skit John Pratt waves to wife Sheila Craig, mermaid daughter Terry Johnson as he is rowed to work.

At The Red Barn. (See caption.)

Red Barn, 1950. Cast members Gladys Forrester, choreographer, dance instructress, and lead dancer, beside Sheila Craig, revue actress, with Linda Ballantyne, foreground, rehearsing.

I thoroughly enjoyed my summer at the Red Barn. It was hard work with no time off, but we were young and enthusiastic. I was a little cross with the stage crew, who failed to secure the three steps leading from the dressing room area to the stage. In one of the four shows, I had fifteen costume changes and, in my hurry to make it to the stage, I did a running approach to the steps and often fell. By the end of the season, I had bruises all over my left hip ranging in colour from dark blue to purple and, finally, yellow, but there was zero tolerance for complaints. This was summer stock theatre in 1950. We had to be tough.

Brian Doherty, our producer of the Barnstormers, was staying in the 140-year-old Sibbald family residence. The Sibbalds owned the entire point and had invested in the Red Barn Theatre. Also staying in a Sibbald property with Brian Doherty, although only briefly, was Susan Fletcher, accompanied by theatre critic E. G. Wanger. Susan was the niece of Vincent Massey, chancellor of U of T, and Raymond Massey, a well-known Hollywood actor. Susan was twenty-nine, very good-looking, and a stage veteran. She wrote most of the lyrics for a very racy number performed by Donald Wolvin, probably with some input from E. G. Wanger. Although E. G. Wanger, or Ernest Wanger as he was then called, had written several reviews, we had never met. I only saw him in the distance. He was bald, although very tall and well-built with a handsome profile. Susan and her escort also wrote lyrics for some of the other numbers.

There were parties at least once a week, hosted by the affluent cottage owners who were delighted to entertain the Barnstormers. The chief of these were the Sibbald family. At one of these parties, I lingered, talking with the hosts, and suddenly found there was only one other guest left, a rather substantially built dark-haired man. He seemed pleased to offer me a lift. I believe the hosts assumed he was connected to the theatre, and I thought he was a friend of the hosts, so I accepted. It turned out that he was neither. The moment he pulled out of the lane, he pulled out a bottle of whiskey, took a few slugs, and offered it to me. I wasn't happy about this, but I decided to play along as if I was keen. I pretended to drink the whiskey and heard my driver telling me he wanted me to go and spend the night at his cabin. I was terrified but said that sounded like a great idea. Then, pretending to drink some more, I announced that I needed to grab my toothbrush and a few things I needed for my rehearsal the next morning. I asked him how far away the cabin was because I had to be able to get back by ten in the morning for my rehearsal. I can't imagine I was that good an actress, but since he was somewhat drunk, he seemed to fall for my act. He stopped at my old hotel, let me out, and I ran like hell, praying that the outside door was still unlocked. It was, and I never looked back.

The balance of the summer of 1950 went very well until a few days before the end of the final show. The most popular numbers from the first three shows were chosen as the nucleus for the fourth and last show. My fellow actors and I noticed that our talented and creative director was drinking excessively. The closing number in *One for the Road* was a rousing number with wild dancing and lively music. I was dressed as Miss Canada in a white bathing suit with a scarlet sash and my red dance shoes, which, by this time, were losing their colour. I had just attempted to repair the damage with red lipstick. After the show, I was tired and went to my room and lay down on my bed, still in costume but with a newspaper under my shoes, leaving the door slightly ajar so my delightful roommate, Anne Wickham, the tall dancer in white in the Casino Theatre skit, would enter knowing I was already in. Within no time, my door was opened, and a very drunk Roy Wolvin entered and more or less threw himself on me. I reacted instinctively, pushing him off with my shoes. Not a word was said, but later I wondered what the cleaners thought when they were handed the off-white men's trousers stained with lipstick.

BURLESQUE ON BURLESQUE is done by lugubrious singer Jack Northmore, bored chorus girls and dancer Ann Wickham. Called "Kasino Theatre" skit, it was one of the revue's top hits.

Chorus Lineup, *Burlesque on Burlesque,* with Ann Wickham in white, fresh from New York performance, and my roommate, later a close friend. (See caption.)

I had been looking forward to the last week of August and early September when our Barnstormers were to perform for the hotels in cottage country. I was not invited. The situation with young actresses and directors, sadly, in some jurisdictions has not improved.

It was time to write a sup and because I was now at liberty, I had a little time to study. I wrote the exam and did rather well. But I was at loose ends and wanted to earn a little money. Someone told me at the last minute that there were jobs still available at the Canadian National Exhibition, which was about to open. I heard that the food truck rally had signs offering employment, so I headed down to visit the site and offer my services. There were posters in front of some of the booths offering various jobs. One that caught my eye was a booth offering a job for someone to call out the benefits of Norval's malted milk. I thought this was an opportunity for me as an actress, so I attempted to apply. I was told that they were looking for a man. Having just spent two months performing in a variety of roles, including singing and dancing (I was neither a singer nor a dancer), I asked them to let me audition anyway, and since I persisted, they let me audition. I was handed the script and a mike and within five minutes was offered the job. As the exhibition was about to close, a rugged-looking man in his forties approached me and asked me to come to his booth at closing. There he offered me a job to go on the road as a barker with the carny. I would be a performer in a carnival. I thanked him but told him I had another job lined up.

I finally graduated from university. Chancellor Vincent Massey handed me my diploma. I smiled at him, but he was stoned-faced.

128 Growing Up in Toronto "The Good"

John Howe and me, graduating—John Howe in the spring of 1950 and Sheila Craig in the fall of 1950.

Part 3

Royal Conservatory of Music and Opera School, 1951–1953

Chapter 10

In early autumn, I was invited to read for a one-act play to be presented by the University Alumnae Dramatic Club. When I arrived for the audition at Barbara McNabb's apartment on Wellesley Street, the director, whom I had never met, was none other than E. G. Wanger, the drama critic. He cast me as Doña Clarines, a Spanish baroness, the title role. He cast Bill Hutt as my brother. This was the fourth time Bill and I performed together. It turned out that E. G. Wanger's real name was, in fact, Ernst Waengler. In mid-twentieth century Toronto, a name like his was far too foreign for its citizens, almost entirely white Anglo-Saxon, to accept. True, there were ethnic groups, such as the Italian, Greek, Portuguese, Jewish, and Chinese, who liked to live in their communities, but the Northern Europeans seemed to prefer to blend in. Ernst was not typical of any group. He was in his early thirties, born in Vienna to a formerly wealthy industrial family, and, I was to discover, bohemian. *Doña Clarines* was staged in Hart House Theatre, and it was a mild success.

132 Growing Up in Toronto "The Good"

```
              DONA CLARINES                    THE
                   by                          University
                                               Alumnae
         S. and J. Alvarez Quintero            Dramatic Club

    Doña Clarines              Sheila Craig    Producer              Barbara Allen

    Marcela, her niece         Kathleen Knox   Stage Manager         R. V. Jackson
                                                 Assistants          Mary Jury
    Tata, the housekeeper      Agatha Leonard                        Victor Barnett
                                                                     Wilbur Grasham
    Daría, a maid              Joyce Bocknek
                                               Bookholders  (I)      Jane McNally
    Miguel, Marcela's lover    Douglas Ney                  (II)     Christina Templeton

    Don Basilio, Doña Clarines'                Costumes     (I)      Marian Jones
                brother        William Hutt                 (II)     Margaret Munro
                                                                     Barbara McNabb
    Luján, a doctor and Don
                Basilio's friend  Donald Sinclair  Furniture and
                                                   Properties        Jane McNally

           Direction - E. G. Wanger

    Scene: Doña Clarines' home in Guadalema     Saturday Evening, December 16, 1950
                                                       HART HOUSE THEATRE
              Act I  - Evening                    (By permission of the Syndics)
              Act II - The following morning
```

Program for *Dona Clarines* with Director E. G. Wanger.

William (Bill) Hutt, a young actor at UC, University of Toronto.

In 1951, it was decided by my parents and me that I needed more theatrical training. Since my father had a beautiful baritone voice and my voice was also rich but untrained, my father asked his Arts & Letters friend George Lambert if he would give me singing lessons, assuming that I might get the chance to do musical theatre. Mr. Lambert taught voice training at the Royal Conservatory of Music's building at the corner of University Avenue and College Street, which is now the site of the hydro building. George Lambert had a studio there. He was an affable man with a winning personality. He made me relax but I wasn't improving with his tuition. My speaking voice was deep, and it required a long time for me to warm up with scales. Perhaps that is why he decided that I was a contralto. His prize student was a young tenor with an exciting voice, Jon Vickers.

One day, Mr. Lambert asked Jon to come to his studio and sing an aria from *Carmen* as Don José. He asked me to sing with Jon in the role of Carmen, which I certainly wasn't ready to do. Jon Vickers was impressive, even as a novice. I was not. I sang flat, but Jon sang sharp. Jon Vickers became an international star with his powerful, magnificent tenor voice.

One thing that the next two years taught me was how different and international the recently founded Opera School was to anything I'd ever experienced. However, I was intrigued by the totally different atmosphere of the Conservatory from the university.

I wanted to join the Opera School and, in the spring of 1951, I was accepted as a student. There was a decidedly European flavour to it. The first director of the Opera

Division of the U of T from 1946 to 1957 was Ettore Mazzoleni. The first music director was Nicholas Goldschmidt. The first stage director was Herman Geiger-Torel. These names were certainly as foreign-sounding as Ernst Waengler. Mr. Goldschmidt and Mr. Geiger-Torel were both refugees from Hitler's Nazi Germany.

Mr. Geiger-Torel had recently arrived from Buenos Aires, where he'd worked for a few years as a stage manager and where the staging was formal and old fashioned. He was used to singers standing stiffly and emoting. He was a stickler for correct diction and liked to ridicule the English habit of pronouncing words differently than they were spelled. As an example, he cited my name, Sheila, pronounced by English speakers as Sheela. He said, in my opinion, quite correctly, that the vowels should be reversed: "ie" rather than "ei." However, he didn't ask if any of us had prior stage experience. So when he asked me to walk across the stage, I was confused. He then demonstrated and asked me to walk the way he did.

Not planning to be rude, I did just that. The whole class burst out laughing. Mr. Geiger-Torel was not aware that I was somewhat of a mimic, and I'm afraid I had copied his walk, which was leaning slightly to the left. I was embarrassed and Mr. Geiger-Torel looked cross. He said not a word but then asked someone else to walk across the room as if they were on stage.

I enjoyed my new experience. Some of the male students were Eastern Europeans. They were extremely adept with lances and sabres, which the male students were taught to use. The female students were instructed in fencing. In addition, we were all taught how to fall without getting hurt and how to relax and fall down stairs. In the Opera School, all the singers performed in the opera as chorus and citizens, which included dancing.

NICHOLAS GOLDSCHMIDT
Musical Director

HERMAN GEIGER-TOREL
Stage Director

Gina Cigna

Goldschmidt, Torel, and Gina Cigna. Important people at the Opera Division of the Royal Conservatory of Music.

When a small, non-singing role for a woman was needed in one of the operas performed by the Royal Conservatory's Opera School that season, I was often asked to do it.

Several of my fellow students and I were accepted as choristers in the annual Grandstand show at the Canadian National Exhibition. It was good to earn a little money. We performed in the bandshell designed by James Craig of Craig and Madill Architects in 1926 and completed in 1936. It still stands to this day.

CNE Bandshell. Inspired by Hollywood, the Art Deco-styled Bandshell was built in 1936 according to designs prepared by James H. Craig of the Toronto architectural firm Craig and Madill. The building has two-and-a-half dressing rooms, an office, a "green room," a "switch room," and a sound room. The stage is 338 square meters (3,640 sqare feet) in size.

The comic star of that year's Grandstand show was Jimmy Durante of Hollywood fame, with his raspy Brooklyn voice and his large nose. When not on stage, I liked to hang out behind the bandshell with his sidekick, a charming Black man. He told me the marvellous experiences he had had with Jimmy in years past. One day, it was raining, and I approached from the dressing room. Jimmy was with my new friend and said, "Come on up, honey, and join us so you won't get wet." Being the brat that I still was, I said, "Thanks, Mr. Durante. May I stand under your nose to keep dry?" Jimmy was not amused.

Like many comedians, he liked to make fun of his large nose but didn't like it when a lesser person did that.

Jimmy Durante, Hollywood comedian, was the comic performer at the annual Canadian National Exhibition that year. His final comment each evening, with his raspy voice, was, "Goodnight, Mrs. Calabash, wherever you are."

After the exhibition, several of us opera-student choristers were hired as choristers in the pantomime *Babes in the Wood* at the Royal Alexandra Theatre, starring Gisele MacKenzie. I enjoyed performing at the Royal Alex's stage with a professional stage crew and a doorman who greeted me and even said "Good evening, Miss Craig."

Babes in the Wood (See caption.)

The Opera School had a choreographer, Gweneth Lloyd. This was essential because most classical operas require some members of the chorus and, occasionally, the professional dancers on stage. I was one of those chosen. My partner for the European dances, especially the Wiener Walzer and the polonaise, was a good-looking, young baritone, Robert Goulet, from Quebec. We made an attractive pair. In 1960, I was jealous of his sudden rise to stardom, thinking how much easier it was for male performers to get ahead since there were so many more roles for men than women. He's the only person in my life I've ever been jealous of.

The year 1951 was a very busy one for me with the University Alumnae's winning entry of Bernard Shaw's *In Good King Charles's Golden Days*. It was directed by the *Globe and Mail*'s drama critic, Herbert Whittaker. I played Nell Gwynn, the mistress of King Charles. John Colicos won the Best Actor award for his portrayal of the king, and our play was chosen as the best play of the Dominion Drama Festival.

Saturday Night magazine cover from 1951, with John Colicos as Good King Charles in *Golden Days* and Sheila Craig as Neil Gwynne.

Herbert Whittaker, director, receiving the award for the best-directed play in that year's Dominion Drama Festival.

> **Nell And The Duchesses**
> Sheila Craig as Nell Gwyn and Ruth Norris and Marian Jones as the Duchesses of Portsmouth and Cleveland respectively, are handsomely costumed for the University Alumnae Dramatic Club presentation of Shaw's "In Good King Charles's Golden Days." Play is being given tonight at the Arts and Letters Club.

Two duchesses and Neil Gwynne. (See caption.)

In March, I played the American Houseguest, my first ingenue part, in the International Player's production of *The Chiltern Hundreds*. I didn't enjoy the role. I found my character boring, even if I did look right.

Then came professional radio. I loved the fact that it was live in a studio with the director in the control room giving signs to either speed up or slow down. I did thirty-two weeks of Ford Theatre for Alan Savage, but I especially liked working with Esse Ljungh. Later I got a contract to do a series of twelve radio sessions of *Songs of the British Isles* for Keith MacMillan, son of Sir Ernest MacMillan. I was to sing four folk songs, writing and speaking an introduction for each one. I received a thirteen-dollar payment per show. On one occasion, I was overwhelmed when Glenn Gould, Canada's star classical pianist, walked into the control room, sat down, and listened until I finished my song. Since nothing was recorded, everything was live. I had to watch the control room if the time was running out for my cue to finish.

Television first came to Toronto on September 6, 1952. I felt intimidated about approaching a director for a role. The TV directors came from commercial radio backgrounds. They were unlike my university directors. Somehow, I didn't feel comfortable and remembered what my father would say: "Promote an idea but not yourself."

Back at the Conservatory, I got to meet members of the faculty. The newest member was Gina Cigna, a handsome woman in her fifties who had been brought by Ezra Schabas from Milan, where she was the head of the vocal faculty of La Scala, the famous opera house. She was tall and striking with sparkling dark eyes. At the time I didn't have any idea that she had been a famous diva who sang the roles of Norma, Tosca, and Aida in Europe's prestigious opera houses. After my less-than-illustrious start as a singing student with George Lambert, I didn't dare ask to make a change. However, I got up enough nerve to ask Madame Cigna if she would accept me as a student. When she first heard me sing, she screwed up her face and said, "Ugh."

Diva Gina Cigna greeting the Royal Conservatory's singing students.

Had I known at the time what an amazing person she was and how she had thrilled thousands with her glorious voice in the past, I don't think I would have had the nerve to ask her to teach me. However, since she had, as yet, no other students, she agreed to take me on and was extremely patient. She taught me how to breathe from my lungs and expand my diaphragm, and she congratulated me on my prowess. But she had more difficulty retraining my voice. After a while, when I improved, she informed me that I was a mezzo-soprano with a potentially wide range, but that I had a great deal of work to do.

In the late fall of 1951, Dora Mavor Moore invited me to meet her at her home in a stuccoed-over log cabin a few blocks north of Eglinton, two doors west of Bathurst. I asked her about this fascinating bit of early Canadian architecture, which was so out of keeping with its neighbourhood, a 1940s middle-class mainly Jewish area of one and two-storey brick dwellings with some small apartment buildings on Bathurst Street. Mrs. Moore told me a little history of her unique dwelling. Situated in the hundred-foot lot, there was an ancient tree overlooking Ridelle and a long unpaved driveway leading to the one-and-a-half-storey house. It seems that in 1837, the leader of the rebels, an enemy of the Family Compact and other elite families in early Toronto, then known as York, took refuge in Mrs. Moore's house. He was William Lyon Mackenzie, a journalist and politician who founded newspapers critical of the elite. He led the rebels after his third feat in the Upper Canada Rebellion when the government troops overwhelmed them in the Battle of Montgomery's Tavern. On December 7, 1837, Mackenzie was forced to flee and took refuge in the cellar of 2 Ridelle (a narrow space with a ladder-like makeshift stairway). William Lyon Mackenzie's grandson was William Lyon Mackenzie King, Canada's prime minister during the Second World War.

William Lyon Mackenzie, 1795–1861, journalist and politician. He founded newspapers critical of the Family Compact (elite families in early Toronto known as York) and led the rebels in the Upper Canada Rebellion. Mrs. Moore informed me that he took refuge in the cellar of what was now #2 Riddell, her residence, after the rebels' defeat by government troops at the Battle of Montgomery's Tavern (December 07, 1837). His grandson William Lyon Mackenzie King was Canada's Prime Minister during the Second World War.

Later in 1951 Dora Mavor Moore invited me to audition for the English director of the New Play Society's production of *Peter Pan* to be performed from December 26, 1951, until January 10, 1952. Peter Pan was a role I had longed to play ever since Mary Martin played it off-Broadway in New York. My competition was Toby Robbins, a favourite of Mrs. Moore's and a popular CBC performer. After a long session that included flying off and on the fireplace in Mary Martin's loaned harness, the director and Mrs. Moore had a rather heated discussion offstage. I couldn't help overhearing the conversation. The director favoured me, but Mrs. Moore insisted on having Toby since, as she said, Toby was better box office. Mrs. Moore won out. I was so disappointed, Mrs. Moore agreed that I could perform the role for the matinees. The day of the first matinee arrived. As I was about to put on my costume, Mrs. Moore informed me that she couldn't afford to pay for the stagehands to rehearse with me briefly, so I wouldn't get to perform. Of course, I was devastated. I have to admit that Toby was a charming Pan, but I would have been Peter, the boy who never grew up.

When Mrs. Moore told me I would understudy everybody, I felt like walking out, but I agreed and did go on for Mrs. Darling. I resented having to learn the roles of all the female cast and not even get a credit on the program as the understudy for Peter Pan and the other women's roles.

In *Spring Thaw* 1953, I was once again told to understudy Anna Russell, the lead. One day I was told that I would have to go on that night because Anna had laryngitis and she would appear to mime the singing parts. I would sing the music, which would include her riotous opera takeoffs, which appealed to me. As I was rehearsing an hour before opening, Anna arrived and, after hearing my rich mezzo-soprano voice, decided that she would perform herself. So much for being an understudy. It is not the most rewarding of occupations. However, the memory discipline is certainly very useful training for stage.

About this time Mrs. Moore knew that she was paying me too little. I think she realized that I was about to request a salary raise because that evening I received a large bouquet of roses in the dressing room from her. I was reminded of her saying, "We are professional theatre, not commercial theatre."

A short time later, I had a call from Dora Mavor Moore asking me if I could borrow my father's car and pick up a gentleman at the University Club. She added, "I have invited him for dinner. I will invite you as well. Mr. Guthrie is the gentleman's name. He will attend the fire, I will cook, and you can serve." Father was pleased to loan me the car, and I was happy to oblige. I found Dora's guest quite charming, and we got along very well.

The talk between Mr. Tyrone Guthrie and Mrs. Moore was all about theatre, and Shakespeare in particular. I was reminded of the hours I had spent with my vocal coach, Mrs. Baker, reading passages from Shakespeare, and how I had welcomed these sessions. After the first course, when Mrs. Moore was getting the dessert, Mr. Guthrie said, "You know, I like the way you move. You have a fine stage voice. I'd like you to read for me." But before I had a chance to answer, Mrs. Moore, arriving from the kitchen, said, with her rather British accent, "Oh Tyrone, Sheila is a *singah*." Mr. Guthrie answered, "Too bad, I'm only using male voices."

I was speechless. There seemed to be nothing more to say. It began to dawn on me that the woman I thought of as a mentor considered me only as a useful tool in her quest to be the mother of Canadian professional theatre.

During the twenty-minute drive from No. 2 Riddell to the University Club, I was longing to contradict Mrs. Moore, but remembering my upbringing, "don't promote yourself," I remained silent. Needless to say, I never got to enjoy the circular stage as a performer at Stratford, Canada.

James Mason, Tom Patterson and Tyrone Guthrie. Photo by Peter Smith.

When the railway industry pulled out of Stratford in the early 1950s, journalist Tom Patterson had an idea for breathing new life into his native city's economy: a festival of Shakespearean theatre.

James Mason, Tom Patterson, and Tyrone Guthrie.

THE NEW PLAY SOCIETY

ROYAL ONTARIO MUSEUM THEATRE

100 QUEENS PARK

Founder and Director - Dora Mavor Moore

April 26th, 1952.

To Whom it may Concern:

It gives me much pleasure to state that I have found Miss Sheila Craig a gifted actress, a pleasing personality and most intelligent.

Miss Craig has at all times been most conscientious, adaptable and has shown an appreciation of true artistry in her performances, both as singer and actress.

I would strongly recommend her as one of our most promising young Canadians.

Yours truly,

Dora Mavor Moore

Dora Mavor Moore's letter regarding Sheila Craig, and a photo that Sheila took of Ms. Moore's house at #2 Ridelle with Sheila's father's car.

Granted there were other acting and singing opportunities, including a wonderful offer from my beloved singing teacher Madame Gina Cigna, who approached my parents for their permission for me to go with her to Milan and live with her while she furthered my training as an opera singer.

One may wonder why I turned that down. There were two reasons. The first was that I believe an opera singer, to achieve recognition, requires first the voice, then the stage presence, including physical appearance, and the ability to project to the rear of the theatre, all of which I basically had. But I was lacking in two very important ingredients. I was not a true musician, and I was not devoted enough to work very hard.

The final reason was that I had met the man I was to marry. I was now grown up.

Acknowledgements

I wish to thank my nephew Ronald Taylor Tasker for providing me with photos of my family and a comprehensive history of our ancestors which he compiled.

As a novice writer, I wish to acknowledge the guidance and encouragement of my editor Beth Kaplan.

I also wish to thank my friend Shalah Sherrer of Print 123 for scanning and digitizing the many photographs.

The small pastel sketch of two-year-old Sheila was purchased by my mother for 50 cents. It was drawn by Dorothy Stevens Austin (Canadian artist) at a fundraiser which took place at the Grange, part of the AGO in Toronto.